WHO CAN STOP THE WIND?

MONASTIC INTERRELIGIOUS DIALOGUE SERIES

Who Can Stop the Wind?

*Travels in the Borderland
Between East and West*

Notto R. Thelle

Translated by Brian McNeil

LITURGICAL PRESS
Collegeville, Minnesota

www.litpress.org

Dedicated to the memory of the Socratic Buddhist,
Keiji Nishitani (1900–1990)

Cover design by David Manahan, OSB.

Originally published as *Hvem kan stoppe vinden? Vandringer i grenseland mellom Øst og Vest,* Universitetsforlaget, Oslo, 1991 (since 1995 Oriens Forlag).

1   2   3   4   5   6   7   8   9

Library of Congress Cataloging-in-Publication Data

Thelle, Notto R., 1941–
    [Hvem kan stoppe vinden? English]
    Who can stop the wind? : travels in the borderland between East and West / Notto R. Thelle ; translated by Brian McNeil.
        p. cm. — (Monastic interreligious dialogue series)
    ISBN 978-0-8146-3329-8 — ISBN 978-0-8146-3934-4 (e-book)
    1. Christianity and other religions—Mahayana Buddhism. 2. Mahayana Buddhism—Relations—Christianity.   3. Christianity and other religions—Japanese.   4. Japan—Religion.   I. Title.

BQ7436.C57T5413 2010
261.2'4392—dc22   2010017167

Contents

Faith in the Border Zone

In this book, the "borderland" is the place where faith meets faith. Faith tends to be formed and lived out in a world with safe borders: we know the landscape, we know the proper place for everything. Faith's travels can indeed lead us to new panoramas and depths we ourselves had not imagined; but others have been there before us and have registered these sites in faith's cartography. It is good to be here.

But some people leave home, cross the borders, and travel in a new landscape—perhaps because they are unhappy and long to get away, perhaps because they are adventurous and curious. Others leave home because they have received a commission, or think they have.

Those who cross the borders and live in the border zone where faith meets faith quickly discover that their world changes. The landscape is unknown, and the local language is different. New friends share their experiences and their insights into life. The world becomes larger. But that is not all. The landscape of one's own faith looks different, when seen from the perspective of the border zone. Something hard to define happens en route.

This book attempts to share thoughts and experiences generated by my encounter with the religious traditions of the East. I crossed the borders because I had a commission: I was to invite others to take the path of my own faith and to see if it was indeed possible to take this path in other landscapes. This commission led to a fresh orientation as I traveled along new paths in an unknown country.

I lived in the border zone for sixteen years, in close contact with Japanese Buddhism and other religions. For most of this period, I worked at the ecumenical Center for the Study of Japanese Religions in Kyoto. My task was not only to study religion as an academic discipline but also to come into contact with the *life* behind the external forms, rituals, and dogmas. I was challenged to reflect on whether Christianity had any message for people who traveled along other paths. I made new friends who drew on sources of which I knew nothing, and I asked myself whether these had any connection with my own sources. I was forced to reflect on how faith could be lived in the border zone—for that was precisely where I and many others were! How could one be faithful to Christ while at the same time preserving the rich cultural traditions that had been formed by other religions? It was a unique privilege to work in the missionary tradition elaborated by Karl Ludvig Reichelt, the Norwegian missionary who did pioneering work among East Asian Buddhists: we were expected to encounter other religions and cultures with an unreserved openness and empathy, and our task was not only to preach the truth but also to search for the truth. In this way, I became a kind of pilgrim. I could not reproduce a world of faith that would be a perfect copy of my own landscape back home. Nor could I retreat to a safe distance on my own side of the border, shouting across to the members of other religions on the far side.

I had to set out on my travels in the border zone. I followed my Buddhist friends into their world. I took off my shoes—like Moses before the burning bush—because I stood on holy ground. Sometimes I discovered that the ground was very far from holy, but that was no reason to abandon my desire to let my friends take me into their own "holy of holies."

My faith bears the marks of my travels in the border zone. My friends made profound impressions on my way of thinking. They shared their wisdom with me and showed me their dreams; they led me to sources I did not know and gave me new visions. Some of these friends, named or unnamed, have their places in the story I shall tell here. They taught me something about the gift of friendship.

Occasionally, my travels brought me out into the borderlands of belief itself, and I began to wonder if I might not be crossing over into a region without faith. At the same time, however, the whole journey was a journey inward, into faith. Sometimes, in my fumbling attempts to see more clearly the contours of the mystery that is glimpsed only dimly as in a mirror, I failed to find what I sought—God hid himself in clouds and darkness. But there were also lightning flashes of insight, in which I saw fragments of a divine reality so intensely alive that I will always continue to seek to see God more clearly.

I am no stranger to inner conflict. On the one hand, I have a message to communicate; I am meant to guide people and give them the right answers. On the other hand, I too am one who searches. What does one do when the trails disappear and the answers remain hidden? Sometimes my Buddhist friends gave me answers that were truer than those of my Christian brothers and sisters. Sometimes my explanations were meaningless, because they offered answers to questions that no one had put; I had to lay them aside and try to formulate questions that were meaningful for both sides in the dialogue.

I am also familiar with fear. I have dreamed that I was running naked along the streets, searching for a place to hide—or that I stood in the pulpit in my underwear, trying to get hold of the manuscript of a sermon without a proper conclusion. I am afraid of being exposed, of being weighed and found wanting.

I have met people who saw through the half-heartedness and emptiness in my life, and that experience is always humiliating and hurtful—and yet, because they believed in me and were able to coax forth something better in me, such encounters gave me fresh courage. I am convinced that that is how God works, and this encourages me to write.

I am not one of those who looks for authoritative answers undergirded by a felicitous concordance between theology and reason. Behind all our explanations and answers, there await other questions and new puzzles. My own relation to truth is intuitive: truth comes to me like a quivering joy when I suddenly *know*, beyond any possibility of refutation, that I am in touch with Reality. It is as if I recognize something that I had always known, but not yet consciously discovered. True questions have given me greater joy than intelligent answers, for the questions open up a vista of new landscapes, whereas the answers seldom live up to what they promise—especially so, when they claim to be definitive. Instead of solving our puzzles, answers can close the doors, leaving us to wander helplessly down futile labyrinths.

Those who are looking for a tidy synthesis and unambiguous conclusions about what happens to faith in the border zone may be disappointed, and some will say that this book consists of fragments and loose ends. And perhaps they are right! But they would have misunderstood me if they refuse to trust me and ask whether I really am a believer at all. Most of what we say about God consists of fragments of a reality that cannot be grasped in our concepts. And I am aware that even the most apparently orthodox façades can often conceal an abyss of confusion and suppressed doubts.

Often, we fail to see the larger pattern. Life is made up of fragments—something we are permitted to understand in intense moments of clarity. But these rare glimpses of the larger coherence are possible only because we sense that the fragments too contain a pattern and a meaning.

The short chapters in this book could perhaps be read as letters from the border zone. Most of them are in fact love letters, reflections that share my experience of leaving home and of longing, of paths and of travels, and of the homeward path.

Confidence or trust is not a quality we "possess"—it comes into being when we choose to trust another person. This book is written in the trust that the reader will accept my invitation to accompany me into the border zone.

Setting Out on the Journey

One who crosses geographical borders
has in fact taken only the first step
on the journey away from well-known, safe surroundings.
The great departure takes place
when our own world is challenged,
when the internal borders are opened
and we undertake a new orientation
in a larger universe.
Abraham set out from his country
and began his travels out into the unknown,
to the country God had promised him.
It is not for nothing that he received the name
"father in faith."
His faith was shaped by his journey.
He met the Lord in the unknown.

"Tabi" means journey or wandering;
it is a theme popular among pilgrims and poets.

TABI

"Who can stop the wind?"
(Kobo Daishi)

"The wind blows where it chooses,
and you hear the sound of it,
but you do not know where it comes from
or where it goes."
(John 3:8)

Who Can Stop the Wind?

When Kobo Daishi (774–835), one of the great masters in Japanese intellectual history, renounced the power and luxury of the court and its bureaucracy and set out on his wanderings as a homeless monk, his family and friends thought he had gone mad and they protested loudly. His reply was simple: "Who can shatter my resolve? Who can stop the wind?" These words were more than just an appropriate metaphor for an irrevocable choice—they described a whole way of life. Kobo Daishi was whirled up out of the secure framework of his life, and he let himself be carried along by the wind. He had seen all too clearly the emptiness of the "good life" and he knew that he could find a more authentic life only if he encountered reality without any protective clothing. He could perhaps have drowned out this call and shut out the wind, but he knew that it would just keep on blowing. As a man of the spirit, he had no other choice.

When Jesus talked with Nicodemus late one night about being born anew, he too pointed to the wind: "The wind blows where it chooses, and you hear the sound of it, but you do not know where it comes from or where it goes. So it is with everyone who is born of the Spirit" (John 3:8). Here, "wind" and "Spirit" are translations of the same Greek word, *pneuma.* The wind blows where it chooses. The Spirit blows where it chooses.

When I was a child, I ran around on a mountain outside Hong Kong, Tao Fong Shan, "The mountain of the Dao-wind." The Dao-wind is the Logos-wind of John's gospel, the "wind of the Word" or "Spirit of truth." Buddhist pilgrims came to this mountain, as did others in search of the truth. Buddhist tradition called these people *yun-shui* (*unsui* in Japanese), "cloud-water." They were wanderers who let themselves be driven by wind and water until they met a master who could lead them to the truth, one who spoke to their hearts and opened their eyes.

When Elijah waited on Horeb, the mountain of God, the first thing he encountered was a storm that split the mountains and broke the rocks in pieces, but God was not in the storm. Nor was

God in the earthquake or the fire. God came in the sound of a gentle breeze (1 Kgs 19:11-13).

It is impossible to halt the Spirit of truth, the Logos-wind. We can indeed attempt to shut it out, building walls and defense-works. We can drown it out with words—our own excuses and the warnings of our friends. But when our words and the ad-monitions of our friends fall silent, we still hear it blowing. It breathes life into words of Scripture that we had not yet discov-ered; it flickers through our dreams and takes us by surprise at unguarded moments. Sometimes it puffs away the mist of our words and in a moment's frightened clarity we know that we must follow it, even though we do not know where it is going.

We have, of course, good reasons to shut out the wind. There are so many winds and so many voices that entice us with their promises about the spiritual life and about fair spring weather, but most winds are deceitful—they die down as soon as one tries to follow them. Other winds turn into storms and we are "tossed to and fro and blown about by every wind of doctrine" (Eph 4:14) until we are left windswept, exhausted, and empty.

But some of this fear is unjustified. We are afraid of what we do not know. Some people are afraid that they may be led into faith—they are modern and secularized and have become ac-customed to look on the church and Christianity with contempt. Others are afraid that they may lose their faith—they do not want to risk being blown away from a childhood faith in which they no longer really believe and being led into a more adult faith and insight that they do not yet know.

We know it is the Spirit of truth who is blowing into our lives, but we resist it. Yet in our heart of hearts we know that no one can stop the wind. It does not let go of us as easily as the false winds—it keeps on blowing. Surely we are not going to let fear of the unknown prevent us from following it on its path. Who can stop the wind?

Faith's Companion

Why is it so difficult to make doubt faith's companion? Instead of meeting it face-to-face and welcoming it as our traveling companion—a companion that tests the genuineness of our faith—we make it an outlaw, and it roams around as an unseen menace, sneaking in like an anxious foreboding in the blood or an infectious sickness in our innermost heart.

You wake up one morning and are aware that someone has been there, leaving behind traces. But you dare not admit that your guest in the unprotected hours of the night was doubt. All you sense is fear—fear lest doubt might tell you that you have set your hopes on something that never became wholly real in your life.

But there is another fear too, a fear that leads you one day to open the door just a little and let doubt come in. This is the fear of inauthenticity.

In the obscure riddles of your dreams, you have already tried many times to tell your heart of your distress. The earth on which you stand is cracking up, and the convulsions are so violent that there is no safe place for your feet. You go from room to room in your childhood home and try to set fire to the furniture. You are on a ship tossed by the waves, and you are terrified of the unknown forces that pull you downward.

One day, you open your eyes and know with perfect clarity that you cannot go on concealing the truth from yourself: you are drifting, and you do not know what is happening to all that "faith" of yours.

Many veils had to be whisked aside before you yourself understood what was happening, before you grasped that you might perhaps be on a course heading directly toward unbelief. What will people say? What will your friends think, or your father and mother? Perhaps you utter a silent prayer that your faith may hold out at least until your father and mother are dead, so that they will be spared the grief and disappointment.

But once you have set the door ajar and taken the risk of this frightening encounter with doubt, the truth knows no quarter—and now you are in the eye of the storm.

As a child, I never tired of hearing my father's dramatic stories about typhoons over Hong Kong. Every time, we were astonished by the strange interplay between the forces of nature and the ten-thousand-tonners. The vessels that cut their moorings and put out to sea, into the teeth of the storm, survived; but some of the boats that remained in harbor, attached to their anchor chains and their moorings, were left as rows of wrecks along the harbor wall.

Sometimes, God calls people to go out into the storm, where they must sink or swim—better to capsize with honor than to be hurled against the harbor wall and crushed!

Now the storm rages over you. But after you have been whirled around by unknown forces for some time, life takes on a new meaning. Precisely at the point where you fear that the powers of chaos would suck you down into the depths, you realize something of which you had never before been completely certain: you believe.

In reality, these words are misleading, since doubt does not assail us like a squall of wind from outside ourselves. All you have done is to open a door to some of the abysses within yourself and unleashed these mighty forces. You are a helpless collaborator in their work of destruction. And then the miracle takes place, just as on the first day of the creation: out of chaos, newly created life is born.

Faith as Fate and as Choice

Many years ago, in the late 1950s, one of the pioneers of the Norwegian Humanist Association held lectures on the nature of religion in the cathedral high school in Oslo. The sham of Christianity's claims had been unmasked, and the debate was in full swing. He concluded one of his talks with these strong words: "If you had been born in China, you would not have been a Christian. You would have been a Buddhist or a Daoist or a Confucian!" These words really struck home! Those of us who were members of the school's Christian union exchanged alarmed glances as we sat sweating on our chairs.

I was the next to address the public, and I held the shortest—and most successful—speech of my life: "Well, as a matter of fact, I was born in China." Everyone knew that I was the chairman of the Christian union, and the whole assembly hall burst out laughing. Every subsequent contribution to the debate was completely irrelevant; the evening was a defeat for the humanists. All their arguments faded in view of the irony of fate that had made me the living proof of the error in their thinking.

But although the humanist's words were drowned out by laughter that evening, this naturally did not mean that his questions had been answered. I do in fact suspect that his question was primarily rhetorical; he wanted to weaken our confidence in *all* religions, rather than to challenge us to be open to the knowledge offered by other religions than our own. Nevertheless, let us put the best construction on his words. He was challenging us not to take our inherited religion for granted. He wanted to sow doubt about faith as a "fate." The historical accident that one was born in a "Christian" country is no guarantee of the truth of Christianity.

My thoughts have often returned to that debate. In the first place, it taught me that "victory" and "defeat" in debates are not always decided by a neutral evaluation of the arguments put forward and of the respective weight of the positions held by the debaters; the outcome is just as much dependent on the speakers' elegant language and ability to formulate their thoughts, on their wit and irony, on the impact made by their personalities, or on coincidences such as the one I have just described. And second, of course, I subsequently had to admit that the speaker was right: if you are born in the East, it is highly improbable, statistically speaking, that you will be a Christian. Religious adherence is largely determined by geography.

This is a very simple fact that need not unsettle our faith. On the contrary, it can force us to think through our faith, and it can whittle away ingrained but superficial ideas that take the superiority of Christianity for granted.

When I returned to the Far East, where I had spent my childhood, I felt the magnetic attraction of the local religions. In such a situation, faith could never be just a matter of course. Here in Europe, however, the situation has changed, since it is no longer exclusively the humanists or atheists who issue challenges to our faith. Buddhists and Muslims and adherents of other religions are active in all Western societies, and they are beginning to change the face of Europe.

An English friend told me recently that of the two hundred thousand citizens in his hometown, fifty thousand are now Muslims or Hindus. There are not so many in a country like Norway, but they are certainly a visible presence. We ought perhaps to get accustomed to the idea that a monopoly on *Weltanschauung* no longer exists: there is no longer one majority religion. Rather, societal development means that a plurality of worldviews and religions is now normal.

The sociologist Peter Berger has analyzed this transformation in modern Western societies. In the past, religion was determined by one's "fate" in the sense of one's historical and geographical circumstances. Today, the world into which we are born obliges us to choose in the sphere of faith, and Berger speaks in this context of the "heretical imperative" (from the Greek *hairein*, "to choose"). The plurality of religions and worldviews forces us to set out on our own journey and choose afresh. In modern Western societies, it is just as likely that one will abandon Christianity as that one will discover a living faith. Indeed, it is possible that an acuter sensitivity is required, if one is to choose faith rather than to drift away from it.

We can therefore take the argument put forward by the humanist in my high school in the 1950s and reformulate it as a challenge to new generations not to take inherited attitudes for granted. For example, we could say: "If you had been born in Africa, you might have been a Christian! The fact you were born in a country that is in the process of forgetting its inherited faith does not permit you to presume that Christianity does not lead to a truer and more integrated life."

The Death and Resurrection of Our Words

During my time at high school, I was fascinated by Ibsen's description of the emperor Julian the Apostate in his play *Emperor and Galilean*. The young ruler is portrayed as a zealous witness to the faith who seeks to defeat the old religion by undermining it from within. He wanted to conquer the teachers of pagan wisdom by sitting at their feet, following them into their own world, and wresting the weapons from their grasp:

> Wrestling with the lions! . . . It is God's will that I should seek out Libanios [the teacher of wisdom]—worm from him his arts and his learning—strike the unbelievers with their own weapons—strike, strike like Paul—conquer like Paul in the cause of the Lord!

I myself had been interested in Buddhism for many years. The Norwegian missionary Karl Ludvig Reichelt did pioneering work in establishing a new attitude toward the religions of the Far East. He saw Buddhists as searchers for the truth and friends on the "path" (Dao). He entered fully into their world, adopted their way of living, and admired their ideals. He was convinced that the deepest ideas and expectations in Buddhism pointed to Christ, and he believed that his vocation was to lead Buddhists "on internal paths" to him who was the Way and the Life.

Reichelt's visions became an integral dimension of my dreams. Like the young prince Julian, I wanted to enter the world of Buddhist wisdom, wrest their skill and learning from them, and "strike them down" with their own weapons. In my youthful zeal, I did not reflect all that much on the historical fact that it was Julian himself who was conquered by the pagan wisdom and became "the Apostate."

It was a shock to discover that I was completely unprepared for my encounter with Buddhism. It is, of course, true that there is a lot of watered-down piety in Japan, a Buddhism based only on customs and superstition—if you want to write about "the darkness of paganism," there are rich materials on which to draw! But if you possess eyes and ears, you gradually also discover depths of faith and religious experience that not only present a *positive* challenge to your faith but also amount to an *onslaught* on it.

When I arrived in Japan, I brought with me much of the best in Norwegian Christian life. I had grown up in the strict tradition of the church's pietism, which was, nevertheless, fairly generous and tolerant. My own home had been permeated by a genuine faith and commitment to missionary work. I went to Sunday school and attended services in the local church. A number of years of intense activity in the Christian union in my school were complemented by perspectives from the Student Christian Federation which *was* open to a broader cultural inspiration. This was followed by solid theological studies, accompanied by the usual crises—doubt, uncertainty, and finally clarity.

Like most students, however, I was "unfinished" and immature when I left the theological faculty. I was able to expound Scripture, I was familiar with the church's history and teaching, I had a basic theological training, and I was capable of developing all of these resources. I also possessed a number of weapons with which to respond to objections and criticism. But I still had a long way to go.

I quickly discovered that my Norwegian background had not equipped me to encounter Buddhism in a meaningful way. It was not that I lacked theological knowledge; as a matter of fact, I knew quite a lot about Buddhism, and further studies would deepen this knowledge. What was missing was the dimension of *depth* in my faith, something that would be capable of encountering what Rudolf Otto has called the "almost incomprehensible experiential world" of Mahayana Buddhism.

The only way forward was to set out on my travels, seeking to penetrate more deeply into Buddhism, hearing the meaning that lay behind the words, and grasping the life behind the outward forms. I sought closer contact through conversations and studies. I have had overwhelming experiences both in spiritual dialogues with Buddhist friends and in simply being present in silence while they *worshiped*. From time to time, I myself took part in meditation under Buddhist masters.

I shall never forget my first meeting with a Zen master in Kyoto.

"Why have you come here?" he asked. "You Christians too have meditation and prayer!"

I answered that we did indeed possess these things, but that I wanted to see Buddhism from within; and Buddhism surely had something to teach us Christians too.

"But why on earth are you so keen to learn about Buddhism—or indeed about Christianity?"

I must admit that I no longer felt quite so self-assured . . .

"It is raining outside tonight," continued the master.

We sat in silence and listened. The rain fell gently on the moss and herbs in the monastery garden. Then, suddenly, there came the impossible question:

"Is it Buddhism or Christianity that is raining?"

My thoughts darted around in the silence. But the rain gave me no answer.

"It is quite simply raining," he observed. "This is a question of *being.* All your theoretical thoughts about Buddhism and Christianity are separating you from the simple and fundamental matter: *to be.*"

This was the first time it dawned on me that faith could separate me from life, or rather, that speculations and pious explanations could build walls that shut out reality. Perhaps my faith would have to be demolished if I was to become a true Christian? And if the encounter with Christ did not help me *to be* in a way that was true, had I in fact encountered him?

One day, the master told me how I should enter the hall of meditation: "When you go into the hall, you must lay aside all your thoughts and ideas and concepts. Leave your theology behind you. Forget God!"

I pondered these words. Is this possible? And is it right? Eventually, I concluded that this paradoxical action could be profoundly Christian. A Buddhist too must lay aside all his ideas—about Buddha, about enlightenment, about the path to salvation. He must (as it were) abandon Buddha at the entrance to the meditation hall. But the first thing he does on entering is to bow reverently before the statue of Buddha in the hall: he must forget Buddha, but Buddha is there. A Christian must lay aside all his theology and bid God farewell outside the meditation hall. But God is there when one enters—as near to us as our own breathing and heartbeat.

This master had studied the Bible, and one day he put me to the test:

"The Sermon on the Mount says that we are not to worry about tomorrow. What does that really mean?"

Innocently, I began to tell him about God's loving care for us. He is our father, and we are the children he looks after.

"I know that," he interrupted. "But what does it mean?"

I attempted to express myself more clearly: "We believe in God's providence. We have nothing to fear. Jesus compared this to the lilies in the field and the birds of heaven . . ."

Again he interrupted me: "Yes, I know all that, but what does it mean?"

Gently but ruthlessly, the surface of all my explanations was peeled back to reveal mere theology, theories, and empty words. He was not interested in explanations, but in the reality itself. How could I express without words the Christian's lack of worry?

Suddenly, I recalled the first Christian testimony I had ever made. I was about fourteen years old and assistant leader of a patrol in the boy scouts. My older brother was in high school and had begun to master the pious vocabulary, since he was an active member of the school's Christian union.

"It isn't difficult at all," he said. "Just read a verse of Scripture and say a few words."

I believed him and selected a verse that I liked and read it to the patrol: "Consider the lilies of the field. Look at the birds of the air. Do not worry about tomorrow." Now I was supposed to say something, but the words would not come. All I managed was a helpless mumbling, to the effect that: "Um . . . the Bible says . . . ah . . . that we are not to get worried . . . that means . . . um . . . ah . . . I think. . . ." I had fallen victim to a pious deception on the part of my brother! I was not much more than a child, but I was expected to be an adult and to represent God: "It's easy, just say a few words."

And once again, now in the Zen temple in Japan, I experienced the collapse of my words. But this time, it was not just the pitiful and embarrassing experience of a fourteen-year-old. What was at stake was nothing less than my Christian faith!

In the course of many years of study, I had learned how to use words and concepts and to combine them to form a theological whole. This house had a beautiful façade, but its furnishings were borrowed from others—from my childhood home, from churches and meeting-houses, from theological libraries and lecture halls, or from books. I had built a house for others, but only a part of me lived in it. How incredibly naïve to believe that I could bear witness to this Buddhist master about the Christian's lack of worry and about God's fatherly care! He saw through me. He knew that I was uttering words that were fully alive only in my brain, and to some extent in my heart—but they did not live at all in my kidneys and intestines and heartbeat and respiration! Nevertheless, it was good to experience this, since the master did not intend to expose either me or my Christian faith. All he wanted to do was to scrape away the hollow explanations and pious words in order to get into the very marrow and uncover the naked heart.

In Zen, words must collapse if we are to encounter reality. This is a painful process, because it opens the door to fear and despair. Zen speaks of "the great doubt" and "the great death"; it is only after these that "the great faith" comes. Some Buddhists whom I have met believe that this is the same as "the dark night of the soul" in the writings of St. John of the Cross. After you have experienced the crumbling and disintegration of your words, you can no longer frolic in words and figures of speech with the same superficial enthusiasm. And you become attuned to the silent dimension of faith.

Buddhism too is full of words. The collection of its sacred writings in Chinese runs to one hundred enormous volumes, and it is impossible for any one person to get an overview of all this material. The foundations here are the narratives of the

Buddha's life, but there are so many versions and legends and apocryphal stories that it is not easy to identify the historical kernel. In addition, there are philosophical speculations and discussions, commentaries on these texts, and an endless series of commentaries on the commentaries. There are also guidelines for ethical conduct and guides to meditation and spiritual exercises.

Despite all these written documents, Buddhism remains unshakably aware that what *really* matters cannot be said in words. "Buddha proclaimed his teaching for fifty years, but never said one single word," it is claimed; we are told of Buddha's "thunderous silence" when he refused to answer those who were curious about the reality that lies beyond the realm of sense perceptions. Buddha did not teach a knowledge that is primarily accessible to the intellect. He taught a truth that can be grasped only in an illumination that breaks through all barriers and transforms the person's life. Daoist wisdom makes the point with exaggerated emphasis: "The one who knows does not speak. The one who speaks does not know." In the words of D. T. Suzuki, the great missionary of Zen Buddhism in the West, "The crux is how to communicate the silence without abandoning it." He himself wrote tens of thousands of pages about Zen, but he never forgot that, on the deepest level, all this was merely beating about the bush.

The most beautiful expression of this insight is the narrative of how Buddha found the one who would bring "the light of the teaching" to others. One day, Buddha sat in front of his disciples, lifted up a lotus blossom and spun it round silently in his fingers. They all waited eagerly for the message he would give them; only Maha-Kashapa smiled at this revelation, for he had grasped the wordless truth that lies beyond all doctrinal propositions and traditions. And it was he who received the commission to bring the light to others.

As a Christian, I believe in the Word. "In the beginning was the Word, and the Word was with God, and the Word was God. . . . And the Word became flesh and lived among us" (John 1:1, 14). I read God's Word and preach the Word. I believe that, for all their poverty, human words can express divine things that shatter the narrow frameworks of our words. But the Word who was in the beginning, Christ who is the heart and the true meaning of God's love and wisdom, did not come to us as a *word*: the Word became *flesh and blood*. The Word did not come as theories and explanations and abstractions: the Word was a child in a manger, one human being among others. He healed the sick, proclaimed freedom to captives, ate with sinners, gave the poor a new dignity, died on a cross, and rose again from the dead. He told parables and stories. He laughed and cried. He shook his fist against hypocrisy, and he danced with children. His "kingdom of God" was no theory, but a new reality that came into being among the people he encountered.

Jesus' disciples followed the tradition he had begun. They proclaimed God's love by telling about what Jesus had done. In this way, the early church continued a Jewish biblical tradition: just as Israel had borne witness to God's greatness by telling the story of how they were liberated from the house of slavery in Egypt and entered the Promised Land, the Christians told about God's love by relating the story of Jesus. The gospels were not written as texts to be interpreted and expounded by preachers and scholars: they are *themselves* the message about God's deeds. In their utterly simple stories of deeds and events, in symbols and images and parables, the gospels reveal how God is.

In our Norwegian Lutheran church, many people have seen that the *Word* has been transformed into *words*—the "church of the Word" became a church that produces huge quantities of words. Sometimes we speak as if we knew everything about God. We describe God's being and his characteristics. Theologians walk a tightrope between various heresies when they seek to define the Trinity or analyze the two natures of Christ. Priests and preachers speak of "God's will," though others can discern only a struggle for power, an opinionated insistence on the correctness of one's own positions and personal ambitions. Carl Gustav Jung once observed that theologians talk about God in a "shameless" manner, and I believe that there is a similar bashfulness deep in the souls of our own people when it is a question of the things of God. We theologians employ too many words; we "know" too much.

I am not saying that words are meaningless. Language is a wonderful instrument that can point to a reality beyond the boundaries of words. But it is too easy for us to succumb to a superstition about words and concepts, forgetting that there is indeed an *unutterable* dimension that lies beyond all our words. The mystery is situated between the *word* and that which is *un-said*. It cannot be contained within our systems, it can only be praised in stuttering human words. If we are too keen to analyze it and define it, it crumbles away between our fingers.

The true problem for the Christian church is not that our words are crumbling into dust, but that our innumerable words are choking and killing the mystery. Perhaps it is the grace of God that lets our words die in order that we may seek that which is real.

It is, of course, true that some people find that their faith crumbles away when words lose their meaning, but often this indicates that their faith had already disintegrated; it was merely held together by a tight corset of words and formulae. Many people experience the exact opposite, namely, that although the words may die, the mystery itself lives. Indeed, both occur simultaneously: the words crumble away and the mystery is revealed in a new clarity. And subsequently, there is a profound joy when the words rise up from the dead! This resurrection of our words need not mean that it is easy for us to find the words we seek; our words may perhaps become fewer than before. Now that we are more attuned to the mystery, we know that no words can explain it—all they can do is point to it.

Among the things I found most fascinating in my encounter with Japanese culture were the simple black and white brush drawings. A few strokes of the brush created a full picture, lacking nothing—a flower, a reed, or bamboo—simple, yet vibrantly alive. The picture is created not only by the strokes of the brush but also by the untouched white surfaces of the paper.

When we describe our faith, we often want to fill out every last detail of the picture. Perhaps we ought to take the risk of

simplicity: a few strokes of the pen, a few words and hints, so
that the white surfaces can come alive and the words can bear us
further out, across the boundary of our words, into that silence
where God's mystery is vibrantly alive.

Adversaries—and Allies

Before I left for Japan, I had a conversation about "mission"
with a fisherman in northern Norway. He was the chairman of
the local group that supported missionary work, and he wanted
to know what kind of religion the Japanese had. I told him that
most of them were Shintoists and Buddhists and that I myself
was particularly interested in Buddhism.

"Buddhists?" he said, after a pause, drawing the word out
slowly. "Tell me, what are 'Buddhists'? Are they the same sort
of people as Baptists and Methodists and so on?"

I gave him a little information about *Buddhism*, enough for him
to grasp that this was a different religion from Christianity.

After a new pause, he brought out the unambiguous deduction
from what I had said: "Aha! I see! So you are *against* them!"

I do not remember my reply to this; I suppose that I tried to
make him understand that although I desired to communicate
the message of my own faith to the Buddhists, this did not necessarily make us adversaries.

In one sense, this conversation did not lead anywhere; but in
another sense, it taught me something important. Our conversation came to a dead end because I had allowed the wrong question to dictate what I said. Once we see mission as an activity
directed *against* others—whether we call them pagans, Buddhists,
Hindus, Muslims, or humanists—the situation gets distorted and
they become adversaries. The world is split into two, and the
alternative is a simple *pro* or *contra*—truth or falsehood, light or
darkness, God or Satan, good or evil. Obviously, it follows that
we must fight against other religions and undermine them!

The fisherman was enthusiastically committed to Christian
missionary work; but we should note that on this point, he took

the same position as many of the critics who accuse missionaries of cultural imperialism, aggression, and prejudices. They too see the proclamation of the Christian faith as something destructive—Christianity can flourish only on the ruins of what went before.

Both the fisherman and the critics overlook one essential point, however. Although there is much that separates Christianity from Buddhism and other religions, as human beings we are first of all allies, united in the attempt to discern meaning in a chaotic world.

We believe, each in our own way, that we have discovered the most important answers. Naturally, these can contradict one another. A Christian will not conceal his faith in God, the Creator who loves his world, who discloses his love and makes it an effective reality in Christ, and who leads us by the Spirit; and the prospect of sharing this faith with others fills us with joy and enthusiasm. But this does not prevent us from listening to the others. A new world is disclosed when we abandon our defense mechanisms and take the risk of touching the deeper yearnings and the unsolved puzzles. Our position changes, and we discover a genuinely spiritual fellowship that transcends all our boundaries. In some sense, we are on the same side.

And this entails a transformation of our understanding of missionary work. When our defense mechanisms crumble, a new sense of security emerges. As a Christian, I do not need to defend the Lord God; nor do I need to undermine other religions and worldviews. Mission does not mean winning victories over others, but rather encountering allies in a vulnerable openness. The words we employ take on a searching quality as we listen and ask questions. Our words become intriguing and dangerous. Our thoughts wrestle with those of others. Faith is shared, and faith is put to the test. Life encounters life.

En Route

The traveler finds friends who share their insights
and open the path to new vistas.
The world becomes larger.
At the same time, one's own world
is put into perspective.
Unknown heights and depths become visible.
The voyage into another faith
is also a voyage into one's own faith.

"Fûkei" means landscape, vista.
It is made up of the signs for "wind" and "vista"

FÛKEI

"The Son of Man has nowhere to lay his head."
(Matthew 8:20)

Even at the end of the road
my dreams wander
over the desolate moors.
(Haiku by Matsuo Basho)

Where Do You Stay?

One of the shortest conversations in the New Testament took place in the desolate desert tracts east of the Jordan. Two of the Baptist's disciples walked behind Jesus to find out more about his message:

> [Jesus] said to them, "What are you looking for?" They said to him, "Rabbi" (which translated means Teacher), "where are you staying?" He said to them, "Come and see." They came and saw where he was staying, and they remained with him that day. It was about four o'clock in the afternoon. (John 1:35-39)

In the East, daily exchanges like this can widen out to embrace the great existential questions; those who are attuned to what these simple phrases can mean know that the words used by Jesus and the disciples are full of meaning. Some of the classic encounters between Buddhist masters and the pilgrims who visit them begin with the perfectly ordinary question, "Where do you come from?" The pilgrim often replies by saying which temple he comes from or which master he has visited. But the real question is: Where have your wanderings led you? How far have you come on the Way?

When they met Jesus and asked him where he lived, the two disciples were looking for the great truth. They followed him to his home and remained with him. This was the beginning of a long wandering, for Jesus did not "stay" anywhere: "Foxes have holes, and birds of the air have nests; but the Son of Man has nowhere to lay his head" (Matt 8:20). Jesus' "home" was a path that led him from place to place. He called himself "the Way." And the first Christians were described as those "who belonged to the Way"(Acts 9:2).

People in the East have a unique awareness of religion as a path; one of the commonest words for religion is *Dao*, which means the way, the law of the universe, the innermost meaning in existence. Buddhism is indeed the teaching of the Buddha, but it is just as much the "way of the Buddha." Daoism is the religion of the Way. Shinto means the "way of the gods." But

Christianity is called the doctrine of Christ, never the "way of Christ."

Japanese often assert that Christianity is difficult. What they have in mind is the Christian doctrine and preaching, which all seem so complicated, indeed virtually incomprehensible! I have often felt compelled to ask myself whether we have turned things upside down. Jesus talked about the narrow path and gateway. He preached a simple message about a difficult path, knowing full well that few would be willing to take it. We have transformed Christianity into an exceptionally complicated doctrine about a way that is so easy that we are tempted to rest on our laurels, thinking that we have already reached our goal.

How often have I heard Christians say that Buddha took the path and pointed to the path, but left it up to each individual to take this path himself or herself! The problem is that when we affirm that Christ himself was the path and that he took this path for us, becoming our "way," we assume that there is no path that *we ourselves* need to take! In other words, we lose our awareness of what "traveling" means.

It is indeed true that Christ took the path for us, but we can pervert this truth into a huge lie if we forget that when he spoke of the "path"—the path that led to his own suffering and death—he was calling *others* to follow him. When he spoke of the cross, he was not summoning others to sit down at the foot of *his* cross! He was challenging us to take up *our* cross and follow him.

In other words, "Christ the way" is a path that one takes, not a place where one "stays."

The Human Person in the Cosmos

In the landscapes of the East, the human person becomes smaller as the world expands and opens up. Some are unsettled, and wonder whether the human person disappears in this vast nothingness. Others, however, stand upright and breathe more freely. Life acquires new dimensions, precisely because it is a part of the great totality.

Chinese artists have interpreted this in their landscape paintings, with endless variations on the classic motif. Mountains tower up and vanish into the clouds, waterfalls rush down over the cliffs past banks of mist and rocks and woods, then disappear into the depths. At the foot of the picture, the landscape becomes calmer, with springs of water and rivers and fields. And it is here that we finally see a human person, as a detail in the mighty cosmos—a traveler, or a farmer plowing with his buffalo.

In a landscape like this, the human person does not encounter nature as an equal partner. To be human means to find and accept one's place in a vast cosmos.

This idea is developed in the great philosophical and religious systems of the East. It is Daoism that speaks most clearly of the intuitive adaptation to the given context in nature: one must live in harmony with the innermost rhythm of the universe, one must listen hard, until one hears the unutterable mystery called Dao (the "Way"). This is not to be found by making oneself lord over things, using knowledge to conquer them and power to manipulate them. The Dao-person, the one who is truly cultivated, is more concerned with wisdom than with knowledge. It is more important to discover one's place in the cosmos than to have a position in the world. The wise person renounces power and does not compel anyone else to accept his or her own wishes and ideas. He or she lets things and events come to pass in harmony with the processes of nature. We find similar visions in Buddhism too: true insight consists in seeing through the emptiness of a self-centered seeking, and the human person discovers his or her true being only as part of a cosmos where all of life is woven together in one great totality.

This perspective has opened up every time I have flown over the vast Asian continent. At first, there is the gray-brown monotony of the deserts in the Middle East, hour after hour. Clusters of houses and towns are etched onto the wasteland, green oases offer small glimpses of hope as they emerge and then disappear again. Life is not something you can take for granted here—it has to be enticed, indeed threatened, out of nature. Then we have the landscapes of the Far East, with an almost overwhelming contrast. As we fly over India, the landscape becomes green, spreading out eastward in an endless carpet of jungles and fertile fields. A warm haze dissolves the sharp outlines. The monsoon climate lavishes its gifts of humidity, warmth, and crops.

The obvious question is how geography and climate shape the inner landscape of human beings. Do the desert landscape and the monsoon climate leave their traces in people's minds and senses and experiences? Tetsuro Watsuji, the Japanese philosopher of culture, is one of many who have attempted to interpret the way people in eastern Asia experience life on the basis of the monsoon climate. He claims that "monsoon peoples" have been formed in a world where nature gives them everything, but at the same time is capable of taking everything away from them. Every year, the moist monsoon winds blow in across the eastern Asian continent, bringing an abundance of water and warmth and growth. The soil is fertile and nature gives virtually unlimited potential for growth so that you can harvest two or three times a year in many places. You can plant a twig in the soil and after a few days it puts down roots and begins to grow. A generous nature lavishes its life-giving gifts unreservedly, and without demanding anything in return.

But the same nature can also destroy the very basis for life. Every summer and fall, the typhoons come rushing in from the sea, leaving a trail of death and destruction, and crushing boats and houses and trees to bits. The typhoon rain is even worse, with floods and landslides and fields laid waste. Millions of cubic meters of cultivated soil are washed into the sea. Another time, it is drought that suffocates life in the fields.

Human beings have no choice when they are confronted with this kind of natural environment, which both gives everything and takes everything away. They have to trust themselves to the environment, come what may. They must find their place in the cosmos and adapt to the great totality. Life is born, and life dies. Nature gives, and nature takes away. It would never occur to the monsoon peoples to make themselves "lords" over the natural elements; their existential wisdom consists in living in harmony with the perennial rhythm of nature.

This prompts objections—is this not all too idyllic? A romantic vision of the unity and interconnectedness of all that lives may perhaps kindle yearnings and inspire the poetic imagination, but reality is surely something more than mere harmony and a feeling of universal unity and the mysticism of nature! What about the almost illimitable poverty and distress in the East? Is it not precisely this harmonious adaptation to their natural surroundings that has paralyzed people's energy and prevented any change? We may perhaps admire the indomitable optimism that endures everything and trusts that life will go on, thanks to the rhythm of nature; but is not the fatalist resignation of the East an even clearer expression of a mistaken adaptation?

Another relevant example is the societal elaboration of the idea of harmony found, for example, in Confucianism, the ideology that has provided the foundations of civil society in the Far East for many centuries. Confucianism has formed the way people shape their life in common and has contributed to social stability with its clear rules about who is higher and who is subordinate, about obligations and expectations. Just as the sky is above the earth, the lord is over the people, the father is over the son, the man over the woman, the older brother over the younger brother. When the lord speaks, the people obey. The one in authority decides, and the subordinate obeys. Critical questions are undesirable, since protest destroys the harmony. It is not for nothing that many have experienced the Confucian idea of harmony as an intolerable straitjacket.

We shall not reply to these objections here, for there is no reason to camouflage the weaknesses in the Eastern visions of the human person's place in the cosmos. And yet, we do well to listen to what people in the Far East say about our own landscapes and about our place in the cosmos. They tell us that we have lost our sensitivity to the mystery of nature. We have made the human person the lord of creation, and we look on nature as an opponent that must be conquered and subjected. Indeed, they remind us, does not our religion state unambiguously that the human person must make himself lord over nature? Is there not a direct continuity between the creation narrative in the

Bible and our own modern abuse of earth and water and fire and air?

Watsuji is one of the most powerful spokesmen for this point of view. He makes an elegant contrast between the monsoon culture and the desert culture, using language with great symbolic power. The unstinting generosity of the monsoon climate allows the human person to discover his place in harmony with his environment, but the desert landscape is barren and niggardly—it is not on the side of life, but is an adversary that must be conquered. Those who live in the desert must fight against the elements, against heat and aridity and sand, in a never-ending hunt for life-giving water and green plants. The natural environment must be squeezed—so to speak—before it yields life.

Watsuji claims that this makes the human person and the natural environment enemies. The struggle against the elements has also formed the three religions that emerged in the desert cultures of the Middle East—Judaism, Christianity, and Islam—and hence has left its mark on the Western mentality. Watsuji is of course aware that the West has been influenced by other landscapes too, not least by Europe's pasturages and arable lands, but he affirms that the desert climate has left its unambiguous mark: the human person in the West confronts nature as an adversary that must be conquered and subjected.

It would not be difficult to call this interpretation of the "desert person" into question. Does not survival in the desert, or in similarly barren environments, demand an extreme capacity to adapt? Only one who accepts the severe demands of nature and lives in rhythm with nature will be able to coax life forth from such an environment. The barren landscape encourages harmony, no less than the exuberant generosity of the monsoon.

Perhaps the real question is whether the adaptation is active or passive. Those who live in a natural environment less generous than that of the monsoon peoples are challenged to use their imagination and their cleverness to discover things that will support life—necessity is the mother of invention. There is no essential opposition between nature and such instruments (nor technology in general). Rather, these instruments come into being through an intimate collaboration with nature. Watsuji's simplified contrast is an unacceptable caricature.

Here too we will not seek to resolve the conflict between the various opinions, since even if these simple contrasts are inadequate as an explanation—or even merely as a description—of the affairs, they nevertheless possess symbolic power. We recognize something true in them, for they reveal tendencies that are clearly present in Western actions and attitudes. Most important, they remind us of insights that are not in the least alien to us, even if we have not, in fact, always seen them so clearly. They inspire us to take a fresh look at the landscape around us and to reflect on our place in the larger context.

I have seldom felt myself a foreigner in the landscapes of the East. I may indeed often use different words, paint other pictures, and interpret things in a manner different from that of my friends. But I have never experienced the Eastern vision of the human person in the cosmos as a *contrast* to the way in which I myself understand the human person's place in creation. On the contrary, my travels in the Eastern cosmos have awakened my senses, confirmed and made clear much of what I knew only vaguely, and opened the door into new insights.

Norwegian piety has tended to isolate the human person in a spiritual universe where the only genuine concern was the relationship between the individual and God. It was a question of sin and grace, of the soul's salvation, of the eternal fate awaiting the individual on the far side of death and the grave. The "Creator" and his "work of creation" were indeed mentioned, but ultimately this was little more than a stage set framing the *real* drama, i.e., the salvation of the individual. The world shrank and became small.

Obviously, this individualistic understanding of what Christianity means is unacceptably narrow. All those who travel in the landscapes offered by the Bible will find larger contexts. The Bible is not concerned primarily with the isolated individual but, rather, with human fellowship. The individual is indeed summoned to act and take decisions, but his or her life unfolds in fellowship.

We are beginning to recover the awareness of the social context of faith. Christians in the Third World have been an important source of inspiration here, since they do not reduce the "spiritual" dimension to a private piety, but have learned from the Master how to articulate their faith in solidarity with the poor, the outcasts, and the oppressed. To be a human person means living in fellowship.

Perhaps we must now go one step further and see what it means to be a human person in the cosmos. The ecological crisis has spurred many to think along new lines. I wonder if the East may have something to teach us here. This was certainly a challenge I met as I wandered in the landscapes of the East, where I discovered something I had always known, something of which the ancient texts speak, something the Psalms praise: God penetrates the entire cosmos with his presence, and the world is full of his glory. I had seen this, as I stood on the mountain plateau and knew that God was there. I had felt it in the vibrations from moss and heather and mountains and woods. I had experienced it by the ocean, where I had my place, with sky and sea and the elements in an all-inclusive totality.

Europeans do not see nature only as an object for research and technology, or a resource for industry and consumption. Nature is also the environment in which we live, a living mystery of which the human person forms a part and by which we are nourished. It is not so very long ago that Norwegian farmers took off their caps in awe every time they went out to sow their seed. When we profess our faith in the Creator of heaven and earth, we locate the human person in the cosmos. How could we be so quick to forget this?

Somewhat paradoxically, we could say that the Eastern philosophies of life, which have no place whatever for belief in a Creator, can open our eyes to profess our faith in God as Creator of heaven and earth. In the first article of the creed, we confess that the cosmos belongs to God, and the human person is given a place in this cosmos. Perhaps it is high time to ponder the consequences of what Paul says: "everything" is created in Christ, through Christ, and for Christ, and "all things in heaven and on earth . . . things visible and invisible, whether thrones or dominions or rulers or powers" were created in him and are to be "gathered up" in him (Col 1:15-20; Eph 1:9-10; Phil 2:9-11). This lets us see something of what it means to affirm God's presence in the world.

The Bible's clearest landscape is the social context, where the human person articulates his life in a great fellowship. But we also see a larger landscape, where the human person is a part of the creation and lives in solidarity with all that God has created. Created things are more than just a stage set for the "real" drama. The second creation narrative in the Bible (Gen 2:4ff.) draws on a marvelous range of symbols to describe how God formed the human person (Adam) from the soil of the field and placed him in a garden. The human person came from the soil and will return to the soil. "Adam" comes from *adama*, which means "soil, earth." The very act of creation expresses the human person's fellowship with all created things. The ancient narratives also say something about the intimate connection between the human person and created things when they tell us that the *ground* was accursed (Gen 3:17) and that the mighty flood destroyed *all life* because of human sin (Gen 6:7). And surely it is important to note that not only the human person but also the animals and the fields are to rest on the sabbath (Exod 23:10-12). In the book of Psalms, created things are not only a passive testimony to the glory of God: they share actively in the universal hymn of praise. Rivers and mountains and trees exult and clap their hands. And the kingdom that is to come is described as "a new heaven and a new earth" (Rev 21:1).

We need a cosmological theology that takes seriously our profession of faith in the Creator of heaven and earth. We must indeed hold fast to the individual's reponsibility precisely as a single person and as a part of the human fellowship, but we must also discover more about what it means to be a human person in the cosmos. As the world opens up in all its dimensions, the human person becomes smaller, both in the East and in the West. At the same time, perhaps it is precisely in such a cosmos that we can stand upright and breathe freely, rediscovering ourselves as a part of the greater context.

Buddha's Path—Between Otherworldliness and Presence

Buddhism seems to begin in a gloomy pessimism and other-worldliness, but it is nourished by a hope that ultimately leads back to the world.

"Everything is connected with suffering," we are told in one of Buddha's classic discourses. Birth is suffering, old age is suffering, sickness is suffering. Everything that makes us cling to life is suffering. We do not need a particularly vivid imagination to envision the poverty and distress in an Indian village 2,500 years ago. Buddha saw the face of pain. He saw through the camouflage and made his pessimistic diagnosis. But he also believed that he had the solution to the puzzle of suffering. This is why his words, for all their heaviness, are colored by hope and expectancy.

The cause of suffering is the blinded yearning that sets everything ablaze. "Everything is on fire," says Buddha in his celebrated Fire Sermon. "The eye is ablaze, things visible are ablaze. All that the eye discerns is ablaze, all it sees is ablaze. . . . The ear is ablaze, the tongue is ablaze, the body is ablaze. It is set alight by the fire of desire, of hatred and of delusion, by birth, old age, and death, by cares, laments, pains, troubles, and despair."

We are tied by desire to an existence in pain—not only in this life, but in an unending cycle of births and deaths. The human person's destiny is formed by *karma*, the inflexible law governing human deeds: every deed entails a necessary consequence that forms that person's destiny. We reap the life we sow every day, and desire is the driving force that ties us to a life of pain. The only way out is to break the bonds that bind us, to extinguish desire, and thus to be set free from the cycle of births and deaths.

Hence, it is not surprising that a central element in Buddhism is withdrawal. The legend relates that Siddhartha Gautama, an over-protected prince, was deeply shocked by his encounter with the dark realities of life—sickness, old age, and death—and decided to leave the world and find an escape route from pain. After six years of hard discipline among the holy men who lived in the woods, he gave up this extreme asceticism and continued his search by means of silent meditation. He abandoned both sensuous pleasure and self-torture, desire and disgust, love and hate. Withdrawn and without attachments he was waiting for insight.

The great breakthrough came after a long night of affliction, when the morning star shone at daybreak. His eye had been purified and was no longer darkened by blindness. The world was still the same, but he came to see things in a new way, just as things take on a new shape and outline in the light of morning. His withdrawal was necessary. It is only when one is set free from the world that one can see what the world truly looks like. Buddha's statues have a peaceful face, an almost invisible smile, with eyes half open and half closed, that speaks more eloquently than any multitude of words about his withdrawn presence. The passion has gone, leaving only an infinite gentleness that does not tie anyone down.

Buddha returned to human society in order to share his insight with others; but all the time, the harmony of his life clearly preserves an element of distance. If it is true that the origin of suffering is blinded desire, then it is clear that one must avoid everything that might stimulate desire. Monasticism became the ideal way of life, with rules and regulations intended to protect the monk against temptations and to make provisions for silence. The classic subjects for meditation were also meant to help the monk see through the emptiness of things in the world and to avoid the ties produced by the senses.

Accordingly, the highest ideal in early Buddhism is the monk who acquires the liberating insight in his withdrawn harmony, breaks out of the cycle of transmigration, and enters the peace of Nirvana, where desire is completely extinguished. It is not for nothing that Buddhism has been accused of preaching flight from the world and an insulated spirituality.

The Buddha's path is unthinkable without withdrawal. But it does not stop there: it leads on into landscapes with new perspectives and vistas, as we see most clearly in the Mahayana Buddhism—the Buddhism of the Great Vehicle—which particularly spread in eastern Asia. Here, we still hear about suffering and desire. The Buddhist sees through the transitoriness and emptiness, but discovers at the same time that the world takes on a new meaning for the one who sees its true form. Escape from the world is not the end; after being liberated, one can return to the world and live a new life.

What perspective opened up the world and shed new light on life? It was no new insight, but a deepening of the central point in the Buddhist interpretation of life, namely, the doctrine of *karma*, the law of causality. Karma offers an explanation of human destiny by locating the human person in an unbreakable chain of cause and effect, thereby also providing the key to change and redemption. This can end up in a self-centered endeavor to break out of the cycle in order to enter the freedom of Nirvana; but this path can also open out onto further dimensions.

If we look beyond the isolated individual and his or her self-centered striving, the doctrine of karma can reveal an interconnectedness in human existence that shatters all boundaries. The teaching of causality is developed in the basic principle called *pratitya samutpada* in Sanskrit, often translated as "interdependence" or "dependent origination." Everything is understood as the result of an endless process of cause and effect. Human beings and animals, things, situations, and phenomena come into being, are transformed, and pass away as the result of an endless network of causes and effects; in their turn, these become the cause of effects in new contexts. Everything is part of this process, from an amoeba to a god, from the tiniest speck of dust to the galaxies in the heavens, from the atom to the atomic bomb. This means that nothing exists in itself, independently of the network of cause and effect. One cannot take one eddy out of a river and look for its innermost substance! Nor can one cut one mesh out of a net and draw up a description of its characteristics in isolation! In precisely the same way, one cannot understand the true nature of things by looking for some isolated "substance" in them. The only way to understand all that exists is to see the entire texture into which it is woven. To borrow the language of the Bible: it is not in God, but in relationships that "we live and move and have our being" (cf. Acts 17:28).

It is this network of cause and effect that explains the transitoriness, emptiness, and pain of things. But it also makes possible a vision of reality that is life-affirming, for if it is true that all things come into being in a continuous process of cause and effect, this means that they are bound together in an unbreakable unity. The various branches of Mahayana Buddhism offer almost ecstatic visions of the unity and interconnectedness of all things, employing both philosophical speculations and the symbolic language of poetry to show us the universe as an organic whole where all things, from the smallest particle to the infinite galaxies, are woven together in a living network. We discover true life when we find our own place in the larger context and play our part in life's great symphony.

This symphony does not consist exclusively of harmonious and optimistic melodic themes high in the descant. There are also deeper notes in the bass, a *De profundis* ("out of the depths") that echoes life's crazy discords. As we hear the voices of life's suffering and pain, the vision of unity and interconnectedness expands to become a solidarity that breaks through all barriers to embrace all that suffers. If there is indeed a unity that binds together all sentient beings, we cannot be isolated from those who live in pain. The condemned of the earth are bound by a thousand ties to the blessed of the earth, and one cannot separate the lives of the unsuccessful from the lives of the successful. In the last analysis, this means that there is no salvation for the individual, for the simple reason that nothing and no one exists in isolation from the totality. The wish to break out and acquire salvation on one's own is an impossibly egotistic dream; the real path to salvation does not lead us out of the world, but back to the world. The world is not denied; on the contrary, we rediscover the world as the place where one can give one's own life to lead *all* life to salvation.

This is why the ideal of piety in Mahayana Buddhism is not the monk who has attained enlightenment and left the world behind him, but the enlightened person who returns to the world to share insight with others there. The highest expression of this ideal is the idea of the *bodhisattva* who, although he has reached the stage where he can leave the cycle of births and deaths and enter the peace of Nirvana, swears by his own enlightenment and salvation that he is willing to renounce this highest good, unless all life reaches redemption along with him.

This, then, is how Buddhism understands the true nature of things. The world is transitory and is in pain. Withdrawal sets one free from ties; but once one's eye has been purified, flight from the world is transformed into a new vision of universal unity, and withdrawal is replaced by a merciful presence.

A classic series of ten pictures, known and loved throughout eastern Asia, offers an eloquent expression of this movement back to the world. They portray the human person's search for his true self as a relationship between a shepherd and an ox. The first pictures show how he seeks its tracks, finds the ox, tames it, and leads it home. He has found what he was looking for.

But the series continues. First, the ox disappears from the picture, then the man too. The identity for which he had longed, and the ego that carried out the search, cease to be interesting. This is indicated by a large empty circle: the world is open. The human person finds the way back to the origin and source of life, symbolized by brooks of water and blossoming trees. It is only in the last picture that the man is seen again, now in the midst of a throng of people in a village square. The protagonist is back where he began his search. Daily life is the same, the people and situations are the same, but the perspective has changed. The one who sought himself has now forgotten himself, and he discovers his true place in the selfless service of others.

"Buddhism has taught me to forget myself," said one of my Buddhist friends. He was nearly one hundred years old, and was trying to sum up the wisdom acquired during a long lifetime. I had discovered long ago that he certainly did not live up to his own words; but then, what Christian believer could ever point to his own self (unless he was blessed with a good sense of self-ironic humor) as an example of the transforming power of faith and insight? After many years in the East, I have never seen more than glimpses and hints of what the realization of the Buddhist visions would mean. To a large extent, Buddhism is shaped by forces that are much more worldly and commercial than contemplative withdrawal and merciful presence! But no one should doubt that the ideals are still alive.

Buddha's path has lost nothing of its challenge. The Buddhism of the Great Vehicle is so demanding that few follow it seriously; even fewer take this path to its conclusion. But Jesus too did not expect that many would follow him on his path.

Buddha's path and Christ's path—the two are described in words so different that one sometimes believes they are located in separate worlds. The strange thing is that they often intersect and that those who attempt to take these paths are surprised to see how much they have in common when they talk about their experiences and share their longings and dreams with each other.

Zen Meditation and the Sacrament of Simple Things

A student once visited the Zen master Gasan in Tenryuji, one of the five great Zen monasteries in Kyoto, and asked him: "Have you ever read the Christian Bible?" Gasan replied: "No—read it for me."

The student opened the Bible and began to read from the Gospel of Matthew: "And why do you worry about clothing? Consider the lilies of the field, how they grow; they neither toil nor spin, yet I tell you, even Solomon in all his glory was not clothed like one of these. . . . So do not worry about tomorrow, for tomorrow will bring worries of its own" (6:28ff.).

Gasan said: "I would say that the man who spoke these words is enlightened."

The student continued his reading: "Ask, and it will be given you; search, and you will find; knock, and the door will be opened for you" (7:7).

Gasan then said: "Wonderful! The man who spoke such words is not far from the Buddhahood!"

A little over one hundred years ago, a Christian theological student called Seitaro Yoshida knocked at the gate of Gasan's monastery and told him that he was "called by God" to meditate under Gasan's guidance. Initially, he did not get beyond the gate, but he did not acquiesce in this harsh rejection—he returned again and again and was literally thrown out of the monastery each time. This is how Zen tests the seriousness and perseverance in a person's religious search. At last, the gate opened, and Yoshida shared the strict rhythm of the monastery's life for three years, before he resumed his theological studies and subsequently became a leading pastor in Japan's Protestant church.

We are not told the name of the student who read to Gasan from the Sermon on the Mount, but it is not improbable that it was Yoshida himself.

Zen or *Zazen*—meditation in a seated posture—is the innermost secret of Buddhism. Buddha himself attained enlightenment in the course of silent meditation. Indeed, many would say that meditation *is* the very Buddha-way. In the silence of the meditation hall, the body and mind become calm, one breathes more deeply and freely, and thoughts become clearer. The life-transforming insight is sought beyond the artificial boundaries of one's thought.

This was the context that Pastor Yoshida entered. He meditated with the monks, worked in the monastery garden and kitchen, listened to the master, conversed with him, and looked for answers to his questions. After three years, he went back to serving the church.

Naturally, this is not a normal career for a clergyman in Japan, and it was even more unusual in the nineteenth century when Buddhists and Christians still regarded each other with suspicion and dislike. Nevertheless, Pastor Yoshida was not unique. He attracted attention because he was a clergyman, but we find the same pattern in many other Christians who were impelled by an inner force to put their faith to the test in the encounter with Zen. They became spiritual pilgrims, setting out on their travels in order to discover the hidden connections in their lives.

What happened to them? And why were they attracted by Zen?

Some who had converted to Christianity now rediscovered in Buddhism the landscape of their childhood, and they turned their backs on Christianity for good. Their Christian faith became just one phase of a path that was absorbed into larger contexts. Others found Buddhism to be so severe and cold that they returned with a new eagerness to the warmth and human concern in the Christian church.

But many—perhaps most—discovered that Zen changed them. Their Christian faith became receptive to Buddhist experiences and insights, and this was more than merely an aesthetic varnish on the surface: new ideas and expressions made their faith look more Japanese. Some found new perspectives on their faith, when they recognized in Zen elements of their own faith; others found that Zen helped them to understand the Bible better, and they spoke enthusiastically of a "Zen spirituality" in Jesus and Paul. Some noticed an inner transformation: their faith was not only challenged and inspired but also acquired a new dimension. They held fast to Christ and remained members of the church, but they believed in a new way.

Something like this happened to another Japanese clergyman, the Dominican Shigeto Oshida. After many years of priestly ministry, he received permission to leave the normal structures of religious life, and he founded a little community in a mountain village north of Nagoya. He says of himself: "I am a Buddhist who has met Christ." He grew up as a Buddhist, and discovered the meaning of life in Christ. Since then, he has lived in the service of the church; but in the course of the years, he has rediscovered a way of life in which Zen is a natural part of the rhythm of faith. Father Oshida does not say very much about Zen, but it is there in the air one breathes, and the visitor notices how Zen inspires everything from worship and meditation and biblical study to the community's meals and conversations and daily work.

Everywhere in the East, one meets "hyphenated Christians" whose faith is formed in close contact with their inherited religion and culture. It seems that the encounter with Zen creates a particularly large number of hyphenated believers, who become "Zen Christians" or "Christians inspired by Zen."

The traffic goes in the other direction too. After Japanese Buddhists overcame their skepticism and grasped that Christianity was not an enemy of the East, there has been a continuous stream of spiritual pilgrims to the Christian landscapes. The Christian faith, and not least the gospel narratives about Jesus, unsettled them and inspired them. They were touched in the very depths of their life experience, and the Bible became their favorite reading, shaping their way of thinking. There are many "hyphenated Buddhists" in Japan. Their existential attitudes are formed by Buddhism, but they are also friends and disciples of Jesus.

What is it about Zen Buddhism that permits Christians to recognize themselves in its experiences, and inspires them to see larger contexts, receive new insights, and be affected in the depths of their faith? The interest in Zen often begins as a romantic and aesthetic attraction. Zen has an atmosphere all its own. Even in temples crowded by noisy tourists, one notices the silence behind the external forms; the architecture hints at hidden dimensions, and the miniature gardens in moss and stone and sand point one to a larger cosmos. Zen has penetrated Japanese art through and through, cultivating existential expressions that range from tea drinking and flower arrangements to sport and martial ideals. In the encounter with Zen, a Japanese Christian who has lost contact with his or her own background is compelled to ask whether God intended that the Christian faith should exclude the richness and simplicity that is at home in the religious world of the East.

Gradually, however, the aesthetic attraction becomes less important as one concentrates on the life that lies behind the forms—the silence, the meditation, the concentration. One quickly sees that Zen makes demands; discipline, will, and perseverance are necessary for meditation. There is nothing romantic about sitting with your face to the wall while your legs ache and your thoughts are unwilling to concentrate. Aestheticism disappears when you are overpowered by sleep, or when you remain dumb because you cannot find an answer to the master's insoluble questions. How is one to meditate when doubt goes about its corrosive work and one no longer knows where all this is leading?

And yet, thousands of Christians continue their journey into Zen because they are nourished by an inner disquiet—which is also an inner certainty. The path into silence does not lead away from their faith, but into deeper dimensions of that faith. All that is superficial is stripped away; one no longer expects dramatic experiences and cosmic breakthroughs, but waits in simple openness. For many Christians, this meditation is a preparation for prayer. Words fall silent, expectations and ambitions disappear, and the mind opens up to perceive a greater presence.

I have helped organize seminars on Zen both for Japanese clergy and for foreign missionaries, and we always met in a Zen monastery. This meant that we not only had lectures and discussions, but could follow the rhythm of the monastery, including the fixed times for Zen meditation. The participants repeatedly confirmed my own observation: Zen can open up paths into silence because it has preserved a unique awareness of the body as an integral part of our spiritual search. Christians speak a great deal about silence and prayer, but they often forget that the body, the breathing, and external circumstances prepare concentration and are themselves a part of the silence. As one participant put it, somewhat paradoxically, "We tend to think that Buddhism despises the body, because it has no place for a Creator. But Zen taught me something about my body that my Christian faith in the Creator ought to have taught me long ago!"

When we hear that Zen is a finger pointing directly to the human heart, and that Zen means discovering one's true self, we naturally ask whether this means that the search in Zen is self-centered. Self-centeredness does in fact flourish in all religions that take the inward path, including Buddhism; but those who are looking for a comfortable ego trip should seek other methods than Zen, for part of the point about finding oneself in Zen is not to confirm one's egotistic dreams but to tear away the mask from the false ego so that the "original face" can emerge. The new world is born when we shatter the artificial world we have built up around ourselves. In Zen, we find our true being only when the ego dies.

This awareness that the true human person is born when the ego dies is a bridge that allows a dialogue between Buddhists and Christians. The conversation reaches a dead end when they formulate their insights in philosophical or theological concepts, but they are speaking the same language when they offer a concrete description of the person who has become what he was meant to be. Here is what one of Japan's leading Zen masters, Dogen Kigen (1200–1253) said to his disciples:

> To get to know the Buddha Way is to get to know oneself.
> To get to know oneself is to forget oneself.
> To forget oneself is to be confirmed by all things.
> To be confirmed by all things is to let go of one's body
>   and mind,
> and to let go of others' bodies and minds.
> All traces of enlightenment vanish;
> and these vanishing traces of awakening must be left behind
>   forever.

Let me mention one further paradox: despite all its emphasis on achieving redemption by one's own power, Zen is profoundly aware that the individual's life is borne up by a greater presence.

There is no doubt that Zen is a path that the individual himself or herself must take. Zen is hard work, concentration, discipline, and a journey toward insight that takes many years. One can listen, learn, understand with the intellect, and receive inspiration, but one must take responsibility for one's own destiny. No one can wake up in place of another person; the insight that transforms one's life is granted only to the person who opens his or her own eyes and sees. The traditional vocabulary calls this "self-redemption."

Nevertheless, those who have genuinely familiarized themselves with Zen have a surprising awareness that enlightenment is ultimately something one receives. The hard work and discipline do not create the insight; their function is to prepare the person and to create a space for the insight. Reality opens up for the one who has let go of his or her own self. There is a link between Zen's demand that one let go of the ego and its awareness that enlightenment is a gift of grace.

The most striking expression I know of this coexistence of hard work and gift is a book of sketches of life in a Japanese

Zen monastery. One drawing shows a monk who at last has achieved his spiritual breakthrough. He has meditated for many months and years, and has given everything to attain insight. One day, the world opens up for him: he is awakened! He reacts to the miracle of enlightenment by stretching out his arms in an explosion of joy—and at precisely this moment, he sees something he had never before realized, namely, that he is sitting on a huge hand, the hand of Buddha. It had been there all along, but I imagine that he did not see it until he woke up and received knowledge. Despite all its emphasis on self-redemption, Zen is conscious that life can be received only by the one who has empty hands and an open mind. This idea is familiar to Christians too.

Zen Buddhism begins and ends with the simplest and most difficult questions of all: What does it mean to exist? How does one encounter life? How can one live in harmony with one's innermost nature? Many people come with exaggerated expectations of ecstatic experiences, cosmic breakthroughs, and superhuman abilities. They may indeed have important experiences, and they may be transformed in the course of time; but Zen does not seek extraordinary or superhuman things. With ruthless consistency, it calls the individual back to the ordinary sphere where life unfolds in its "suchness" or "thusness," as Buddhists put it. Enlightenment means opening one's eyes in such a way that reality can be seen, untouched by desires, ambitions, dreams, and expectations. Zen means finding one's place in reality, not groping blindly for an unattainable dream world, but in a spontaneous and playful presence.

The title of this chapter speaks of simplicity as "the sacrament." It is perhaps somewhat audacious to employ such a theologically loaded word about something as Buddhist as Zen, but I hope the point is clear enough. In the Christian tradition, a sacrament is a visible sign pointing to the presence of invisible grace. The water of baptism and the bread and wine of the Eucharist are fundamental elements of life that become the place of the divine presence in the sacred rites. In Zen, it is precisely the simple and everyday things that have a sacramental character.

There is nothing special about drinking tea, meeting people, going about one's daily work, playing with children, or taking delight in nature; but it is in the elements of ordinary life that the mystery of existence opens up. A Zen poem puts it as follows:

How excellent!
How miraculous!
I carry water.
I cut wood.

Zen does not transcend the human consciousness in a search for "higher" values. On the contrary, one is summoned back to the original awareness, to *this* world. True life finds expression in everyday things. There are plenty of religions in the East that speak of the divinity of the soul and of superhuman experiences, but Zen speaks of something much simpler and much more demanding, namely, of realizing one's own humanity.

Ultimately, it is perhaps this radical simplicity that makes the greatest impact on the Christians who journey into the landscapes of Zen Buddhism. In the course of their search, they become more open to the traditions of their own culture; silence and concentration give them a deeper understanding of the divine presence. Above all, however, they have learned something about true humanity. They have discovered the sacrament of simplicity.

Their Christian background alienated them from aspects of Zen. At the same time, their Christian faith gave them certain advantages, since they had already learned some elements of Zen from the Master himself. He too called people to return to the life they were meant to lead. He, more than anyone else, knew that the true life begins when the self dies. His life displayed what the sacrament of simplicity means. All this led these Christians to read the gospels with a new eagerness, for it was there that they met the true Master who crossed all borders and made the divine presence a reality in people's daily lives.

In very truth, he came from God. But the really miraculous thing about him was his unfailing humanity.

". . . An Open Space in Each Person's Life"

My American friend—let us call him Ron—was not a traditional missionary. He had accepted the advice a missionary leader had given him: "In Japan, you will receive more than you give. But it is precisely by receiving from the Japanese that you genuinely become able to give. You are not going to Japan in order to export the religion of the West. It is not *you* who take Christ with you to Japan. *He* is bringing you there so that you can discover new depths of meaning and learn how you can receive in a new way the good news that God loves the world."

This permitted Ron to meet Japan in complete openness. He had indeed a faith that he wanted to share with others, but he also came in order to receive: "There is an open space in each person's life which can be filled only by a stranger who shares his love and concern with us." This is not the starting point of all missionaries.

The stranger who entered his open space was a Zen master who filled it with his presence. This was not so strange to Ron, since his interest in spiritual questions had initially been kindled by Zen. He had grown up in a traditional American middle class environment, without being involved in church life; but some tragic events during his time as a student made him sensitive to new aspects of reality. He had never grasped what Christians meant when they talked about a personal God, and he felt that Buddhism was closest to his heart. Through Buddhism, he began to be interested in theology, and so his Christian commitment gradually came alive. When his sister converted to Judaism, he was suddenly in contact with three religions at once. His family life involved him in conversations across the religious boundaries.

Ron had mixed motives for his decision to become a missionary. He had met powerful personalities who challenged him to engage in Christian service in the East. He wanted to see his own country from abroad. And then there was his old interest in Buddhism—some questions still awaited an answer.

We worked together for two years and became very good friends. We were both involved in the interfaith encounter. We believed that Christians should let themselves be shaped by their meeting with the traditions of the East. We groped and searched and dreamed of a deeper and more genuine faith. Ron's superiors wanted him to work in the sociology of religion: he was to draw up statistics and questionnaires and analyze the spread and growth of the new religions in Japan. He never really got going on this project, because his main interest was in human beings. He dreamed of combining his academic religious studies and dialogue with pastoral work. His heart was not in statistics and sociology, which remained alien to him.

Above all, Zen was a primary concern, and he went regularly to meditate in Daitokuji, one of Kyoto's great Zen monasteries. He meditated under his master several times a week, and meditated at home every day. There were also intense sessions that lasted for several days, with meditation and work from morning till evening. What was he looking for in Zen, and what did he find there?

The first thing that happened was that he lost his illusions. He had always been a dreamer, although he tried his best to camouflage this. He secretly hoped that he would experience some great spiritual breakthrough, a cosmic transformation— that he would wake up! Later, he commented: "That may indeed happen with some people, but it is very rare. And *I* don't know what it is!"

The disappointment led to doubts and problems, and he was tempted to give up—why should he meditate if he did not attain anything? The Zen master told him that he must meditate without wishing to attain enlightenment, and Ron began to wonder whether "enlightenment" was just an illusion, like so much else in religious experience. When he told the master this, the answer confirmed his suspicion: "That is true. There is no enlightenment!"

This was not just a surprise for Ron; for his Buddhist friends who had committed themselves so profoundly to the search for enlightenment, it was a shock.

The master continued: "But you still lack an answer to your deepest problem as a human being. Who are you? How do you solve the puzzle that you yourself are? How do you break through the wall?"

When Ron said that he could not break through that particular wall, the master went on: "Then who is it that breaks through?"

He repeated his conviction: "It certainly isn't *me*!"

But the master persisted: "Well then, if it is not you, who is it?"

Finally, he wanted to put an end to the conversation and, playing with Buddhist terminology, said: "Not-I."

The master then gave him a new problem to work on, a typical Zen riddle—a *koan*—that he was to solve: "If it is not you yourself who break through, who is it that breaks through?"

He decided to remain, but he had got into a rut. Weeks passed, but he did not achieve anything. After a while, he had nothing more to say, but simply sat in front of the master and repeated his question in silent desperation—and in inner revolt.

Ron is not a man who dramatizes things or embroiders his stories with all sorts of details. But his eyes glow as he speaks about his conversations with the master: "As I sat there in desperation, the master gave me a new question to work on, a new riddle: 'From now on, I want you to breathe Christ,' he said. He talked about breathing the Holy Spirit, about living in one's breath, about breathing Christ." He wanted Ron to understand what Saint Paul meant when he wrote: "It is no longer I who live, but it is Christ who lives in me" (Gal 2:20).

There are not many Christians who have grasped that it can be meaningful to step outside one's own tradition in order to enter more deeply into the Christian faith, and that was precisely Ron's problem—he had never met any Christians who could guide him in this way. His Christian friends gave him many explanations and well-meant advice: "Do this! Read that!" But again and again, he found that their words were not rooted in reality. They were empty.

In the Zen master, he found someone who himself had taken a path. The master expected Ron to find his own path, and he followed him along it.

They met only for brief, intense conversations, but the master *was* there, in a way quite different from any of Ron's Western friends. They had copious amounts of advice, but this seldom amounted to more than words.

Ron is an unusual missionary. He does not succeed in carrying out the role of an "evangelist," yet his search has given him much to share with others. He has taken the path from middle-class America via Buddhism to the study of Christian theology and active involvement in the church. As a missionary, he met Buddhism again, and this encounter put him on the track of new ways to lead the Christian life. He came to Japan with "an open space in his life." He met a stranger who shared his love and concern with him. He found new depths of meaning and discovered how he could receive anew the good news that God loves the world.

Ron has not offered many answers—his testimony is his questions! But his search inspires others to start looking. He is not alone on his journey.

The Priest's "Gift to His Bride"

Another friend of mine, an Italian missionary, once made a film about Japanese worship in which he portrays, with profound sensitivity and empathy, the whole range of Japanese religion, from the silence and simplicity in the meditation halls to the exuberant prayers and incantations of popular piety.

This piety is allowed to speak its own language. The eye of the camera observes the light and colors, and hands and faces and bodies come alive. Music and the soundtrack help the senses to perceive the meaning hidden below the surface. The missionary himself remains in the background. He does not offer any theological evaluations, nor does he divide the various phenomena into "higher" and "lower" religious forms. He does not attempt to show that Christianity is "better" and "deeper" and "truer."

He told me that he would like to employ the film as missionary information—perhaps it could help people understand the deeper sources that nourish the Japanese mentality. God bless him! How could he be so naïve? I can only too easily imagine what many mission supporters would say about his film. They would have objected that it does not contain any "message." They would have wanted their money's worth, arguing that a film about missionary work ought to portray much more un-ambiguously the obscurity of paganism. They would ask what "missionary vision" lay behind the film.

As a matter of fact, the film was generated by a vision. My friend told me how inspiration had come to him. Early one morn-ing, he stood on the beach and enjoyed the sight of the small Japanese fishing boats coming home from the sea. Suddenly, something caught his attention. In the prow of one of the boats, a fisherman bent down and threw some of his catch into the sea, then he stood up, clapped his hands four times, bowed his head, and clapped his hands once more. This is a traditional form of prayer in Japan. Then the fisherman returned to his work as if nothing had happened, and everything went on as before.

But had something happened? The external form was foreign, and the priest could not hear the words that had been said. But the fisherman's simple rite had reminded my friend of the very heartbeat in all true worship: we give back to God something of what he has given us, as a sign that everything belongs to him.

At the same time, he had seen a glimpse of a God who was greater than the church. He was himself a man of prayer, deeply rooted in the church. He was himself a part of the church's life, and I believe that he was in fact a rather conservative priest. He had come to Japan in order to make known to others the mys-tery of faith. But the Christian faith did not shutter his doors: his piety and prayer had opened his senses. He saw God where others saw merely the worship of idols. He wanted to draw the veil aside, so that the others might at least sense what he himself saw—the presence of God.

Some will call him naïve. Did he not see that the religious life in Japan was superficial and self-seeking? Did he not see the superstition and the exaggerated expectations that found expres-sion in the magic of the Japanese prayers and rites? Did he not see the hypocrisy and emptiness? Did he not see the struggle for power and the oppression that lay behind the façades?

He certainly did see all this. After a few years in the country, he had seen more than enough, and he had every reason to be repelled by the rottenness of Japanese religion. As a matter of fact, he had encountered this rottenness most clearly in his own church; and he knew the dark abyss in his own life.

And yet, he painted a sensitive and tender picture of Japanese worship. He was a man in love—something in Japanese culture had touched his feelings and awakened his senses to life. His advances had been reciprocated, and he had made Japan his bride. The film was his "bridal gift," a love poem in colors that spoke of his beloved's soul.

Love had bestowed on him the gift of seeing. He had discovered the human beings behind the abuses and the struggle for power; he had seen the faces behind the masks. He saw that the best and the worst were entangled in the mud, but still touched by God. This did not frighten him, for it was something he recognized from his own life.

This made his film not only a declaration of love for the Japanese soul but also a profession of faith. He had seen the footprints of a God whose kindness and blessings bore witness to him (Acts 14:17). And with Saint Paul, he confirmed the insight of the Greek philosopher who had written these words about God: "In him we live and move and have our being" (Acts 17:28).

The Wide Perspective

For a whole day, our group of pilgrims had been making our way toward the summit. We had gone through cool woods and deep crevices, along precipitous slopes and overgrown paths. The landscape had given us only glimpses of the distant hills and mountains.

Now we had arrived at our goal, and the mist began to lift. Unexpected vistas opened up. It was good to be here, with light and fresh air and unlimited space around us.

This was not just a walking tour. We were pilgrims on our way up a sacred mountain, taking part in a symbolic journey into "the other world," the place of the Buddhas and the gods. We had been following in the tracks of the great masters since the previous day, when we had purified ourselves in the Yoshino River at the foot of the mountain. Ceremonies of initiation and other rites had marked off the various stages en route to the wisdom and light in the world of Buddha.

Our journey concluded with densely symbolic rites on the summit, to emphasize that the search for truth was a question of life and death: one by one, each of the pilgrims was suspended over the sheer drop. Two men held the pilgrim's legs, and a rope was fastened in a loop around the shoulders for safety's sake. As the pilgrims hung over the cliff, they were asked whether they were willing to commit their whole lives to seek the Buddha's path and attain enlightenment.

How ought I to react, if I were asked to make such a vow? I had taken part in the whole journey. The others knew that I was a Christian, and they were happy that I had been there as participant and observer. None of them had told me how I should be interpreting the pilgrimage, and this left me free. This freedom was a gift, a sign of their friendship, and perhaps this was why I felt confident that the master would respect my Christian faith even in this particular initiation rite.

And so it turned out. As I hung over the sheer drop, the Buddhist master asked me: "Are you willing to sacrifice your life in order to create reconciliation between the races and religions? Are you willing to give everything in order to follow your Master, Jesus Christ?" I trembled on the edge of tears. It was a long time since I had been permitted to consecrate my life to him in such a decisive manner.

Would a similar group of Christian pilgrims have had an appreciation of faith and life broad enough to make them open for people who followed other paths, as they entered the innermost sanctuary? I was in a spacious landscape where I could breathe freely, and I realized that it is indeed possible to be spiritual companions even where we do not share the same convictions.

I had already experienced something similar in my encounters with various masters who had allowed me to sit in their meditation halls and had shared their wisdom and life experience with me. They had seen me make the sign of the cross. Their respect for my faith did not prevent them from challenging me and putting critical questions to me. They had scraped away layer upon layer of artificial answers and half-digested theories; they had seen the words wither away in my mouth, so that I fell silent, with no answers to give. But I had never seen any desire on their part to rob me of my faith. They had never made me feel that I ought to exchange the Christian faith for something better, namely, the teachings of Buddha. Their aim was to compel me to descend to the level where things were genuine and alive, to a naked faith that would be like a seed with the potential for growth.

Some may consider this broad comprehensiveness merely a wishy-washy tolerance—does not fidelity to the truth demand that we observe certain boundaries? I must indeed admit that I have sometimes been surprised by the ability of the Japanese to paper over glaring contradictions in order to preserve their highest priority, i.e., harmony and a friendly atmosphere. But that was not the case here. Rather, they were convinced that the path a human being takes is connected to *the* Way. They were confident that the Way reveals itself to us at whatever stage on our journey we happen to be and that fidelity to the Way will lead us to the truth. This insight was so strong and intense that it simply abolished the antithesis between an aggressive missionary zeal and a laid-back tolerance. There was never any doubt about their own position, but they opened their world to others without laying down conditions. They shared their insight without demanding signs of loyalty. They knew that no one could ever be forced to accept the truth; the only way to receive the truth is to take one's own path through life and discover the truth in one's own world.

This perspective is present in our own faith too. We encounter it frequently in the gospel. But when will we realize that God becomes smaller and smaller, the more we try to force him down other people's throats? And that we are in danger of squeezing him out of the narrow structures we have drawn up? God is on his travels through the world. The more we discover the variety of the world, the greater is our appreciation of his presence. We need light and fresh air and wide horizons if we are to find a faith that sets us free.

"The Flower Opens in the Sheer Drop"

There was always someone who was taken by surprise when the shabby old man shuffled into the circle of thinkers and philosophers. His long undervest poked out from his sleeve. He carried some slices of bread in a plastic bag, and occasionally broke off a piece and ate it. He was a chain-smoker. When he began to speak, he groped carefully for the right words. He was not in a hurry; he gave his thoughts time to take shape. He was not eloquent, and his formulations were not particularly elegant. He posed a series of questions that slowly homed in on the subject, and some people wondered what he was trying to say.

After a while, however, something happened to those who listened to him. They were caught in the magic of wondering as he drew them into his own world and filled the room with his presence. This was no longer a closed room, for the walls vanished and the wind began to blow. He was not giving an academic course in philosophy—he was taking his hearers with him on a philosophical journey into reality. And this was highly demanding, because he expected something of his fellow-travelers: they had to take responsibility for their thoughts, and they themselves had to encounter reality. The conversation lasted for several hours, but no one left the group.

The shabby old man was Keiji Nishitani, who died at the age of ninety on November 24, 1990. He was active to the very last as one of Japan's leading philosophers, the most prominent representative of the so-called Kyoto school. I met him in Kyoto in 1972, while I was studying at the Buddhist Otani University, and I had the great privilege in subsequent years of getting to know him in seminars and lectures, formal dialogue encounters, and informal conversations. Few persons have influenced my thinking more profoundly.

Nishitani was a traveler. His basic attitude to life was shaped by Zen Buddhism, and there is no doubt that it was Buddhist concepts that best expressed his ideas; but his travels took him into other worlds too. He studied the Bible, the church fathers, and the great thinkers of the Christian church with a quiet passion, and he taught Western philosophy throughout his long life. His own existential questions were shaped by the existentialist philosophy elaborated by Kierkegaard, Nietzsche, and Heidegger—questions about meaning and meaninglessness, and the problem of nothingness. He took these questions along on his travels and wove them into his own experience of life. One could call him a Socratic Buddhist, one who sought answers and got other people to see by means of the questions he put to them.

When I asked Nishitani to sign one of his books, toward the end of his life, he wrote a poetic greeting that expressed his attempts to discover meaning:

> The flower
> opens
> in the sheer drop

This was not just poetry: it was dearly bought existential wisdom, a profession of faith on the part of a man who had walked along the rim of the sheer drop, had seen the abyss yawning below him, and had discovered that it was precisely there that life's meaning could be seen. "The flower opens in the sheer drop."

Nishitani's travels began with the despairing experience of meaninglessness. In the few glimpses he has given of his own life, he describes his youth as a period without hope, when he was sucked down into the experience of nothingness and hopelessness. He saw his decision to study philosophy as a religious matter, a question of life and death. "In the little story of my soul, this decision was a kind of conversion," he has written. Right up to our last conversations, he maintained his conviction that a true understanding of life is possible only when one is confronted by the abyss of nothingness.

Nishitani was a man of faith. He held that our search for meaning is not a hopeless groping in the dark; existence is borne up by a power that holds all things together, and this power drives us toward the abyss because it knows that it is there we shall catch sight of a new world.

Although it was Buddhism that formed the basic pattern in Nishitani's thinking, he did not wish to be called a Buddhist. Whenever this happened, he felt somewhat embarrassed, and claimed with a perplexed smile that he was in fact searching for something more fundamental, something that lay beyond or beneath both Buddhism and Christianity. The essential point was our shared humanity. What does it mean to be a human being? This is the riddle to which all religions seek the answer. Since Buddhism and Christianity possess treasures of insight, they can help us understand. But Nishitani did not think that any religion had discovered the definitive answers.

Two or three thousand years amount to only a small fragment of history. Must this not mean that religion has an infinite potential to penetrate more and more deeply into the riddles of life? This was the question Nishitani pondered. We must continue our search with an open mind. We must stop hanging on self-consciously to our own principles. We must struggle with life's problems in a radical openness.

Nishitani was most reluctant to let himself be called a Buddhist, but it was even clearer that he did not wish to be a Christian. If pressed, he could say with a smile that he was *en route* to faith; it would be unthinkable for him to *end up* as a Christian. But when he spoke of Christ, his words expressed his love for the great Master whose friend and disciple he was. He had a special preference for biblical motifs, to which he returned again and again. He spoke of God's selfless and unreserved love, about the incarnation as God's "self-emptying," and about Jesus who won life only by giving his life for others. He spoke with warmth and respect even of the idea of a personal God, and he affirmed that belief in God as a person has given special dimensions to our human conscience and love, raising the personality to new heights.

At the same time, however, he was unsparing in his criticism of Christian thinking and of Western philosophy, both of which were held captive in the structures of their ego. The faith in God that the church has inherited has imprisoned it in a universe that will disintegrate in the encounter with science, nihilism, and atheism, he argued. The world does not turn on the axis of a relationship between God and the human person! We must reject belief in God as an absolute deity who rules the world from outside. The attempt to make the human person the center of creation leads to a distorted relationship to reality. What is needed here is nothing less than a revolution.

Nishitani was not a man who raised his voice often, but on this subject he used strong words. He said that Christianity, and most religions, are facing a catastrophic change comparable to what happened millennia ago when the dry land emerged from the sea and many marine animals had to adapt to life on land. Christians must get used to living in a world where there is no longer any God "out there" and where it is no longer possible to understand the human person as the absolute center of activity and thought.

Although he admired Christianity, and not least Christ himself, Nishitani was a severe critic who asserted that there is no future for Christianity in its present form. The solution is not to abandon the faith, but to let something new grow out of the old. Perhaps he envisaged a future Christianity that had been transformed by the encounter with Buddhism?

It is somewhat surprising that a philosopher who was so critical of Christianity should have exercised such a strong attraction on Christians. Apart from his exceptional personality and the inherent power of his thinking, the reason for this attractiveness was quite simply his love for Christ. I shall never forget the time I asked what he thought about what Christian mystics call the "flame of love" in our relationship to God. He sat in silent thought for a while, and then replied quietly, to the astonishment of the Buddhists who were present: "Surely we all need something of that flame."

His criticism came from outside the church, but it was born of his endeavor to penetrate the riddles of life. As a traveler, Nishitani made countless fellow-travelers his friends. He showed them new landscapes and taught them to see, to ask, and to wonder. I never heard him speak of his "disciples," but he had many more than he knew—and a good number of them are Christians.

Now he has laid down his earthly pilgrim's staff; now he is in new landscapes. We still hear the wind blow.

This book is dedicated to his memory.

"Melt, My Heart! Weep, My Eye!"

For many years now, two pictures have accompanied me. The faces of two dying men have looked at me and shared their insights into the mysteries of life and of death.

The contrasts could scarcely be greater: Jesus' ravaged face as he hangs on the cross and Buddha's silent peace as he lies on his side with his face turned to the west. Jesus' mouth is twisted into a shriek: "My God, my God, why have you forsaken me?" Buddha makes his quiet farewell with a few words of exhortation: "All things are impermanent. Work at your salvation." Jesus died a young man, after three years of dramatic activity. The cross came after he had known fear and sweated blood in Gethsemane, after he had been betrayed, arrested, and tried. In his last hours, he was surrounded by enemies, by soldiers, and by a few terrified disciples. Buddha died an old man, after preaching and guiding others for fifty years. On his deathbed, he was surrounded by friends who cared for him and followed him reverently to the border of life.

One could add many more details; indeed, much has been said in illustration of the contrasts between these two death scenes, for the contrast is not just between two personalities, but between two religions. It has been claimed that they are irreconcilable opposites, and the attempt has often been made to demonstrate the superiority of the one over the other; other writers again were content to wonder at the emotional and cultural gulf that yawned between the two religions. Was a mutual understanding possible?

Those Christians who have studied Buddhism over the years have often spoken of Buddha's admirable harmony, even in his encounter with death. They marveled at his heroic aloofness. But at the same time, he was so far exalted above human feelings that he was not really in touch with them. There was something unreal about his death. He took his leave of his disciples with serenity and with firmness: no tie was to bind them to their master, since they themselves had to shape their own future.

In this way, Buddha's death became an image of the greatness in Buddhism, but also of its flaws. It appeals to the will and the thought, and calls people to a truer life beyond their passions and blinded pain, yet is somehow not quite at home in the world. Buddhism never succeeded in changing the world, because it taught that one should be untouched by things and deny the world; its ultimate goal was "being blown out" (Nirvana). Buddhism seemed passive, remote from real life, a religion that denied the world. Its universe was cold, ruled by an impersonal law of life, "having no hope and without God" (cf. Eph 2:12). With his death, Buddha set the seal on his heroic insight—withdrawn and remote, untouched, so exalted that he was almost inhuman.

Those who have even a little acquaintance with Buddhist piety know that this description is wrong. It is indeed true that the Buddhist ideals point away from emotional ties, since all the feelings—from love to hatred—blind the human person and tie him or her more and more strongly to the painful cycle of life. But Buddhism is not cold and impersonal. Its universe is not formed only by impersonal principles; it has an atmosphere that breathes gentleness, mercy, and warmth.

I cannot imagine any stronger expression of the emotional warmth in Buddhism than precisely the many portraits of Buddha's deathbed. According to Buddhist legends, he was surrounded not only by his disciples but also by a throng of animals and heavenly beings, all of whom had come to express their grief at the master's departure. Whereas Buddha maintained his equilibrium and inner calm and pointed away from his own self to the insight that sets people free, all the others—even his disciples, who had followed their master throughout his long life and ought to have preserved the same inner calm—wept unrestrainedly. The paintings depict faces ravaged by woe and pain, and everything that lived took part in this lamentation.

This means that Buddha was more than just an illustration of a cold principle. He had seen through the riddles and opened other people's eyes. He had shown them a world permeated by light and life, a world that lay behind the rigorous regularities governing human actions and behind the necessity for discipline and self-improvement. Buddhists call this mystery wisdom and mercy. The master was the incarnation of wisdom and mercy; and when such a master dies, all life weeps.

Christians have misunderstood Buddha's death; but Jesus' death is perhaps even more confusing for Buddhists, since his dramatic dying in pain and despair seems to conflict with all their ideals of harmony and inner calm. D. T. Suzuki, the great communicator of Buddhism to the West, expresses this reaction with classic clarity: "Every time I see the image of Christ on the cross, I cannot help thinking of the gulf that separates Christianity from Buddhism. This gulf symbolizes the psychological dividing-line between East and West."

Again and again, Japanese friends who have been in Europe have told me how they were overwhelmed by the beauty of our churches—their architecture, their music, their stained glass—and that they sensed the mystery in the sacred room. But why were there always these crucifixes in the center? They found the image of a crucified man repulsive and unaesthetic.

Some maintain that Christians' obsession with the cross is a sign of the sadistic tendency in the West—has not the West always stood for violence, brutality, and aggression? Once again, it is D. T. Suzuki who has formulated this idea most clearly in the "geometric comparison" he makes between Jesus and Buddha. Jesus died in a vertical position on the cross, while Buddha lay horizontally in silent meditation. "Christ hangs helpless, full of woe, on the upright cross. This is almost intolerable to an eastern mind. . . . The vertical axis expresses action, movement, craving. The horizontal axis, as in the case of Buddha, makes us think of peace and contentment."

For Suzuki, Jesus' vertical position on the cross is an expression of the action orientation of the West. The image of one who stands on his feet hints at aggression, self-assertion, power, and exclusiveness, whereas the image of one who lies down denotes peace, tolerance, and broadmindedness. As an active "standing" religion, Christianity is unsettling and deeply disturbing.

Like many others, Suzuki had an ambivalent relationship to Christianity, oscillating between attraction and repulsion. But the emotional repugnance he felt at Jesus' death on the cross was perhaps primarily due to the equation he made between Jesus' life and death and his own particular understanding of the Western mentality. He saw the cross as an expression of Western ideas and attitudes, instead of using the cross as the criterion to evaluate the Western mentality and the way people in the West lived.

This does not mean that Buddhists see only meaninglessness in Jesus' death. Many of them grasp almost by intuition that the path Jesus took to the cross was the fulfillment of the highest Buddhist ideal, i.e., the selfless mercy that sacrifices itself. Many accept the truth of Jesus' call to renounce one's life in order to win life, since this is deeply compatible with Buddhist insights. It is only when the cross is "explained" by means of rational concepts and theories of expiation that it loses its meaning and is reduced to an incomprehensible expression of human brutality and divine sadism.

Just as Westerners need time and guidance in order to recognize the warmth and tenderness in the apparently impersonal and cold universe of Buddhism, so Easterners too often need time to grasp the devotion and tenderness that Christians feel in the face of Jesus' cross and death. If they come with their inherited ideals of harmony and inner calm, the emotional gulf is almost unbridgeable. The contemplation of the cross seems merely a repulsive contemplation of evil and suffering. But if they follow their Christian friends to the encounter with the crucified Christ, they experience empathy with a reality that is very close to them. They discover that Christians are not sadists, that they are not unlike the pious people of the East. Rather, the image of the cross allows Christians to profess their faith in a God who is not remote and withdrawn. In contrast to the somewhat remote presence of the Buddha, Christians see the image of one who entered the lowest depths of human degradation without himself being conquered by this. If we are to summarize the Christian experience of the cross in one word, it is not "aggression" but rather "identification." In the cross, they draw near to the Christ who made himself one with them and revealed himself at the heart of the joy and din and torture of the world.

Undoubtedly, the cross has often been misused and exploited in Westerners' attempts to gain power and to crush others; the most tragic example is the Crusades, which were carried out under the banner of the cross but were surely the most unambiguous *denial* of the cross ever. But we must not forget that down through the centuries, most Europeans have not been aggressors. On the contrary, they themselves have been victims of violence and poverty and all kinds of suffering under the mighty and the rich. The concentration on Jesus' suffering and death was in keeping with official orthodoxy, but for most people, the image of the one who himself suffered and was tempted (cf. Heb 2:18) was more meaningful than the theological dogmas. Jesus, the "man of sorrows," showed them a God who made himself one with human beings. The crown of thorns, the paleness of his face, his tortured body, the eyes that glowed with pain—all this spoke eloquently of *Immanuel*, "God with us."

Surely it is not by chance that Bach's musical style, often unsentimental and "objective," becomes gentle and tender when he tells the story of Jesus' passion in his music and sets Paul Gerhardt's translation of a medieval hymn (here in R. Campbell's English version):

> *O sacred head ill-usèd,*
> *By reed and bramble scarred,*
> *That idle blows have bruisèd,*
> *And mocking lips have marred,*
> *How dimmed that eye so tender,*
> *How wan those cheeks appear,*

How overcast the splendor
That angel hosts revere!

We may compare the words of another medieval hymn, the *Stabat mater dolorosa*, in the free translation by Benjamin G. Sporon:

Who can think of all that pain
Without pain in his heart,
Even if it were a sinner who suffered thus?
But here it was the Most High himself who suffered—
Melt, my heart! Weep, my eye!
See, here it is holiness in person that suffers!

There is no aggression in the music and words of these hymns. They display a tenderness and gentleness that would be unthinkable without a profound inner empathy, indeed a sense of belonging together.

This means that Jesus' death has nothing to do with those qualities Suzuki associated with the vertical axis. Rather, the image of Jesus' death speaks of an identification that brings the vertical and the horizontal together. Traditionally, theology has called this "reconciliation." God's love knows no boundaries but is expressed and made a reality in the most inhuman suffering and evil.

It is meaningless in this context to evaluate the deaths of the two men, Buddha and Jesus. All we need say is that the emotional gulf is not unbridgeable, and that the images and symbols and events that link the last hours of these two men are more important for living human beings than any amount of theories and theological "explanations."

Hallesby and Zen

My Japanese friend had come to the faith by a roundabout path. Originally, he had sought the meaning of life in Zen Buddhism. He hoped that he would discover his true nature through meditation, but he ended up in a labyrinth of self-centeredness.

He continued his search in the Pure Land Buddhism, where salvation was to be found through faith in the grace of Amida Buddha and the invocation of his name. Here he discovered the warmth and devotion he had missed in Zen, the deep awareness of being "embraced and not rejected," and borne up by a power outside his own self.

But it was only in Christianity that he found a stable foundation for his life, in God's love as this is revealed in Jesus Christ.

When he became a Christian, he returned at the same time to his starting point and rediscovered Zen meditation. New doors opened, and his prayer life became richer and deeper. In Zen, with its millennial tradition, he discovered the insight that the body as a whole, with its breathing and its heartbeat, helped bring the mind to concentration. He discovered the falsity in a self-seeking spirituality, and became receptive to a silence that made space for God.

As soon as he heard that I was Norwegian, he asked:

"Do you know a Norwegian theologian called Haresubii?"

"Haresubii? No, I have never heard of him." But after a while, I realized that he was talking about Ole Hallesby (1879–1961). What on earth did a Japanese theologian who drew inspiration from Zen find so valuable in this conservative Norwegian theologian who was famed as a hellfire preacher? Well, he had read Hallesby's book about prayer, and it was precisely this text, along with his own experience of Zen, that had helped shape his spiritual life!

I pondered over my friend's words. There was something here that did not make sense. I did not understand until I actually read Hallesby's book—for here we meet a man who is deeply rooted in Norwegian pietism, but at the same time breaks open its narrow confines. He writes as a pastor; the frontlines of theological debate recede from view, and the harsh words he used in other contexts fall silent. Hallesby draws on a tradition that flows through the whole of the Christian church. This Norwegian pietist becomes a "catholic" in the proper sense of the word, one who belongs to the universal church. His words are in harmony with the message we hear in so many of the church's great masters, from the desert fathers, via the medieval mystics, to Thomas Merton. And a Zen Buddhist too would recognize the truth of many things in Hallesby's book.

Perhaps it was not so odd, after all, that a Japanese who had found the path to the Christian faith through his encounter with Buddhism should discover fresh inspiration in the words a Norwegian man of prayer wrote about the silent life:

> Let the silence work on you. Let solitude work on you. Give your soul the time to detach itself from all that is external, from the multitude of things. Give God time to play the prelude to prayer in your distracted soul. Let your devotion, your sacred passivity, open all the doors of your soul onto the eternal world.

Diamond and Lotus

The diamond and the lotus are Buddhism's foremost symbols for the truth.

The diamond stands for the perfect truth that casts its rays over everything else. Its crystals refract the light, so that it plays in all the colors of the rainbow. As the hardest of all minerals, the diamond is not crushed when it meets resistance. Rather, it cuts through everything.

The Buddhist knows that truth has the nature of a diamond. The truth is perfect, like the most glorious precious stone. It is immutable and cuts through lies and falsehood and darkness.

But if the truth possessed only the perfection of the diamond, it would be almost inhuman—cold and hard and unattainable. In its wisdom, Buddhism points to another aspect of reality: the truth has the nature of a lotus. The lotus sprouts and grows from a tiny seed in the mud, reaching upward to the light. Finally, its blossom opens up in immaculate beauty.

The truth is not only something achieved once and for all. The truth also exists as the potential for growth, and this growth can be delayed and stunted. It is unprotected and faltering—but it opens itself to the light.

Sometimes, another image is used too: the womb. Reality is described as two worlds, the world of the diamond and the world of the womb. One world is complete, perfect, and immutable, and crystal clear like a diamond; the other world has the soft warmth of the womb, with its potential for prenatal growth, for birth, and for growth after birth.

Although each image can be contemplated on its own, they must not be understood as two separate worlds, since they are describing two aspects of one and the same reality.

Perhaps this symbolism can help us look a little more deeply at our own relationship to the truth. When Jesus proclaimed the kingdom of God, he was speaking of something perfect—but at the same time, this was still emerging as a visible reality. He described the kingdom as a shining pearl and as a treasure hidden in the field for which one sacrifices everything. But he also spoke of the kingdom of God as a seed that is sown in the earth and then grows into a huge tree.

I do not wish to press these images too far, but the pearl and the seed can function as symbols in a manner similar to the diamond and the lotus. God's kingdom is a perfect reality; but at the same time, it is still emerging, and we can catch glimpses of it when his word takes root and creates new life, when God touches a human person in such a way that hatred yields to forgiveness, or when violence and injustice give way to freedom and justice. We know that the kingdom is God's perfect gift; but we perceive his kingdom chiefly in its tiny beginnings, as an unprotected seed that germinates and grows toward the light.

As Christians, we believe that the truth is one and that it is perfect: it has the nature of a diamond. We have experienced how its light shone into our lives and cut through falsehood and darkness. Sometimes we even stop traveling and think that we have reached our goal or that we have grasped the truth in its fullness. The faith is crystallized in clear formulations with sharp and harsh edges. We stand there with the diamond in our hands and speak in absolute terms—we have found the answers and solved the riddles. But after a while, we discover that the crystals have stopped glittering and that their surfaces have dimmed.

We try to cut through lies and cheating, but our "truths" have no cutting power. We had failed to see that our little insights and our partial truths were only reflections of a divine reality that we did not hold in our own hands. What we presented as the perfect diamond was only a cut-glass imitation.

We must not forget the other image, the seed that grows. The truth has the nature of a lotus: it lives in us, as a potential for growth, and hesitantly seeks the light. One day, it will unfold as a radiantly beautiful blossom.

The diamond and the lotus are one. The perfect pearl and the seed symbolize one and the same reality: the kingdom of God.

". . . Until the Morning Star Rises in Your Hearts"

A legend describes how Buddha received his spiritual breakthrough after he had searched for many years. Toward the close of a long night of meditation, he finally awakened as the morning star shone at daybreak. He had become a Buddha—an awakened one.

Buddhism is the religion of the eye: its aim is insight, clarity, enlightenment. The great breakthrough comes as soon as the false values fade away in the light of truth. The world is not changed, but one sees its true form, just as things in the world take on form and meaning when the darkness of night gives way to the day.

We are surely justified in affirming that Christianity has had a greater appreciation for the ear than for the eye. Hearing the Word is the foundation of faith (Rom 10:17). The Word is received in obedience, and obedience naturally involves listening. The prophets listened to the voice of God, and they admonished the people to accept the Word. Hearing and obeying the Word are basic characteristics of faith.

The encounter with the religions of the East can make us more aware that faith also sees; we realize that the Bible itself attaches greater importance to this function than we have often done. Jesus taught his disciples to see: "Blessed are the pure in heart," he said, "for they will see God" (Matt 5:8), and it is above all the apostle of love, John, who makes the contrast between human blindness and the faith that sees. Paul speaks of light for "the heart's eye": "Now we see in a mirror, dimly, but then we will see face to face" (1 Cor 13:12). This insight is not some isolated intellectual understanding, but a spiritual insight that accompanies an inner liberation.

It is not for nothing that the church was reluctant to emphasize faith's character as "sight" and "insight," since it did not wish to make a distinction between "ordinary" believers and so-called spiritual Christians, between the obedient hearers in faith and those who appealed to "higher" wisdom and insight. But the church is impoverished if it refuses to acknowledge the need to see with greater clarity. Faith too knows a growth in insight, a movement toward seeing with "the heart's eye."

The Bible has a strange expression that recalls the description of Buddha's spiritual breakthrough. We are told to hold fast to the message of the prophets, which is like "a lamp shining in a dark place, until the day dawns and the morning star rises in your hearts" (2 Pet 1:19). Faith is not only obedience. Faith includes a search for enlightenment, a desire to see with greater clarity and insight. May we not look forward to the day when the morning star rises in our hearts?

Various meditation practices from the East have gradually begun to disturb our one-sidedness. I do not intend to discuss here the validity of their many promises of harmony and world peace; but there is no doubt that this interest in meditation and inner silence has led many people to appreciate new approaches to religion. For the church, these movements have been a timely reminder that there are aspects of reality that our traditional piety has not taken with full seriousness.

It is no exaggeration to say that many spiritual seekers find the church superficial and garrulous; they abandon the church because their religious yearnings find no place in it. They long for the deep dimension of faith, and they look in vain in the church for silence, mystery, meditation—they are not looking for *more* words about God, for better explanations, or elegant formulations! They want to travel into the landscapes of faith, to sense the mystery, and see the inner connections of things.

We live our faith with many senses: we want to hear, but also to see. We need guides who can open our eyes so that the morning star may rise in our hearts.

It Is Dark at the Foot of the Candlestick

Kyoto is the undisputed center of Japanese Buddhism. You can wander through temples and gardens day after day, week after week, and see how history lives in a tremendous richness and beauty. The massive temple halls bear witness to the generations who did their best to create spaces to house their longings. Sculptures and images inspire the pious imagination. Landscapes with trees and bushes, moss and sand, form the perfect framework for the temples whose treasuries preserve the sacred writings, copied and commented on for many generations.

Who could doubt? The light shines brightly, its flame nourished by thousands of years of insight and experience, and pointing the way to each new generation.

And yet, the ancient adage remains alive: "It is dark at the foot of the candlestick." These words sound so innocent and commonplace; but the popular wisdom they express about the center of the religious tradition is harsh. The city with its learning and its temples and its artistic treasures is very impressive, a luminous testimony to Buddhism's greatness—but it is dark at the foot of the candlestick, people remark. Do you not see the struggle for power that is going on behind the walls? See how ambition and pride empty the learning of its vital force. See the pious hypocrisy. Hear the emptiness that lies behind the eloquent sermons.

No, people say—if you want to find a Buddhism that is true and living, you have to leave Kyoto and get away from the learned men, from the center of power, from the bearers of tradition. Go out to the countryside where you can find the simple souls who do not stop the light from shining but radiate it in their lives. You can find the true master in a poor hut just as easily as in the famous monasteries.

Do we not see something of the same paradoxical insight in the stories the Bible tells about God's deeds? Jesus was not born in Jerusalem, the center of religion and of power. He grew up in a poor, peripheral region, and people asked skeptically whether anything good could come from his hometown. Most of his life was lived precisely in that despised province. When he himself stood and looked out over the capital, he wept and said: "Jerusalem, Jerusalem, the city that kills the prophets and stones those who are sent to it! How often have I desired to gather your children together as a hen gathers her brood under her wings, and you were not willing!" (Matt 23:37). Later, when the disciples pointed to the glorious buildings of the temple, he said: "You see all these, do you not? Truly I tell you, not one stone will be left here upon another" (Matt 24:2). It was in the center of religion and of power that he was condemned and crucified.

We see something similar in the story of John the Baptist. Luke describes a scene full of contrasts: when Tiberius was emperor in Rome, Pontius Pilate governor of Judea, and Herod tetrarch of Galilee, under the high priesthood of Annas and Caiphas in Jerusalem, "the word of God came to John son of Zechariah in the wilderness" (Luke 3:1-2). Is it purely by chance that he begins by describing where the great ones in the spheres of power and of religion were located and only then tells us that God chose to act in a completely different place?

For some reason, we appear to need the great centers. What would the world's religions have been without Jerusalem and Rome and Canterbury, Mecca and Baghdad, or Varanasi and Kyoto? What would we have done without places of pomp and authority, centers of learning and sanctuaries, bishops and hierarchs, abbots and caliphs, administrators, lawyers, politicians, diplomats, general secretaries, printing presses and the mass media, or well-oiled and efficient organizations? Is it not precisely these that have kept religion alive? They made religion a player in the power game so that it could shape society. They handed on the tradition, constructed systems, and protected religion against the attacks of heretics from within and enemies from without. They collected taxes so that new buildings could arise to the glory of God. They created culture and gave impetus to architects, artists, musicians, and thinkers. They made religion immortal. Without them, the faith might not have been communicated to us.

Must we accept the necessity of all this? Must we accept that there will never be more than a few who radiate the light of faith, while most of the bearers of tradition carry the light without necessarily living in it? Is not this how human nature is? Must we not adapt to the demands of this world?

Perhaps this is true and right—but I am not so sure. Perhaps the world would in fact have been better without those great centers that made religion immortal? Perhaps the important things happen somewhere else, on the periphery, among the simple people who are despised and forgotten? After my wanderings around Kyoto, this unease lives on in me as a continuous reminder that we often search in the wrong places—for it is dark at the foot of the candlestick.

Reactions to a Message

The encounter between faiths is not
without consequences.
For when the Christian faith is lived
in the borderland,
it will not only be challenged—
it too will challenge.
A living faith does not force itself upon anyone,
but it can be disturbing.
Faith grows and faith withers.
What happens when Christ challenges people
in the borderland between East and West?

"Mu" means nothingness or emptiness.
Like a circle,
nothingness can symbolize that which is empty,
that which is open,
and that which is perfect.

MU

"To find oneself is to forget oneself."
(Zen master Dogen)

"[He] emptied himself,
taking the form of a slave,
being born in human likeness."
(Philippians 2:7)

What a Friend We Have in Jesus . . .

A learned old Buddhist once told me about his relationship to Jesus. As a young man, he had been sent to the university. This period was intended to prepare him to take over his father's responsibilities as priest in the local temple, and he spent his days studying Buddhism and pondering religious questions. One day, he came across a Bible and began to read it. Here he found something that both disturbed him and attracted him—new ideas, new perspectives. Above all, the encounter with the gospels shook him in the core of his being.

"After I had read all four gospels attentively, I was obliged to say to myself: If this is Christianity, then I am a Christian!" He let these words hang in the air for a while, and continued: "But then I traveled to Europe, and I no longer understood anything."

In my encounter with Japanese religion, I have seen a lot of this intuitive love for Jesus. He has shown people the path to what they call *honmono*, that which is unfailingly genuine.

But this love awakens a hope that often proves illusory: when the Japanese seek it in the church that is so proud to bear Jesus' name, they often turn away in disappointment. When my friend traveled to Europe, he could not make sense of what he saw there: where was the Jesus he had met in the Bible? The painful paradox is that many of Jesus' friends in Japan prefer to keep their distance from the Christian church. At best, they can see there a faint shadow of what they have met in the gospels; at its worst, they see the church as a betrayal of Jesus.

What is it that they have seen in the gospels? First and foremost, it is the sacrifice made by love. Christians often summarize the good news in well-known phrases such as "God is love," but I have often heard non-Christians point to Jesus' words about the love that lays down its life: "Unless a grain of wheat falls into the earth and dies, it remains just a single grain; but if it dies, it bears much fruit. Those who love their life lose it, and those who hate their life in this world will keep it for eternal life" (John 12:24-25).

It is certainly not by sheer chance that precisely these words make such a strong appeal. Behind the façade of the modern competitive society, people dream and yearn for love and sacrifice—this feeling may be self-contradictory and unclear, vulnerable and fumbling, but it exists. Sometimes, I have been privileged to meet people who showed me this sensitivity to the sacrifice love makes. When they came into contact with integrity and genuineness, they reacted spontaneously, like the needle of a compass when it enters a magnetic field.

One evening, I sat in the simple rooms of a completely new religious movement and listened to the leader, a twenty-year-old girl. Outwardly, she looked no different from other young people in Japan, but she had an inner radiance and extraordinary gifts. She could read people's thoughts, she spoke in tongues, and she had the charism of healing; last but not least, she was a gifted speaker. I had then—and still have—many objections to the doctrine of this movement and to some of its activities, but I quickly understood that there was something more here than the typical appeal of new religious movements to happiness and success.

She spoke of love and sacrifice. She had no manuscript, but spoke simply from heart to heart. Around her sat sixty or seventy leaders of the movement, young and old, most of them men. She knew that many of them were attracted by the things that happened around her, and she said: "If you have come here in order to experience strange things—ecstasies, prophecies, miracles, and exorcisms of demons—you can go back home again. It is not you that I need. The real miracle takes place when love creates a person anew. I need people who will give all they have, without expecting anything in return. True love will always involve pain. The one who loves others unreservedly will meet opposition."

She drew the listeners into her own magnetic field, and their faces opened up. She touched their deepest dreams: "Our love must not be like the flowers we use to decorate our lives. Our love must be like dandelions. They get trampled on and weeded out, but they do not complain. They just go on blooming, and put forth new shoots. You can cover them in asphalt, but they break open a path to the light. We cannot love without being trampled on. Love leads to renunciation and sacrifice. But we continue to bloom as if nothing had happened."

I have never heard a sermon like it. Her words were quiet and penetrating, shot through with light, and the listeners sat spellbound. They had been in contact with something they knew to be true.

I met another leader of the same movement, who had likewise been drawn into the magnetic field of love. We spoke about Jesus' love and sacrifice, and he affirmed: "It was impossible for anyone who loved so completely as Jesus to become old. He *had* to die—but then, what a fantastic resurrection he had!" This man had never set foot inside a Christian church.

We went on to speak about the path of faith. I admitted how difficult it was to follow Jesus and to love unreservedly. He looked at me and asked quietly: "But is not that the reason we were born? Did we not receive life in order to give it away?" I almost jumped out of my seat and looked at him suspiciously. Was he putting on a hypocritical display of piety? Was he trying to impress me? But no, there was no pretense involved. I sat face-to-face with Nathanael, "an Israelite in whom there is no deceit" (cf. John 1:47). I felt that I myself was more like Nicodemus, who asked Jesus about the new birth and received the answer: "Are you a teacher of Israel, and yet you do not know these things?" (John 3:10).

The dream of love's sacrifice has many variations. It is chiseled in sensitive lines on the faces of the popular saints and gods and Buddhas in stone and wood. It is handed on in legends and fairy tales.

One ancient legend tells of the bodhisattva Kannon (Chinese "Guanyin"), best known as the goddess of mercy, adored and loved by millions in the East. One woman adored Kannon with such a deep devotion that her husband became jealous. One day, as she stood in prayer before the statue of Kannon, he struck her with his sword and left her there bleeding. After a while, she came home as if nothing had happened. Her husband ran in perplexity back to the scene of his crime, and there he saw the statue of Kannon bleeding from a wound.

Why has Kannon appealed so strongly to people in the East? The two characters for her name mean "the one who sees the cry of the world." Her gentle features reveal an infinite compassion. Sometimes, Kannon is portrayed with eleven faces looking in all directions, or with a thousand arms stretched out to touch the whole world's suffering. Does not the people's devotion to Kannon show their abiding awareness of the mystery of grace and mercy?

A few years ago, I was present at the performance of a play in the headquarters of one of the new religions. Five thousand of its adherents were present, and we were fascinated by the simple message of the drama. A princess, fleeing from her enemy, was given shelter by poor peasants in a remote mountain village. It was winter, and they waited in vain for spring—but it seemed that spring would never come. They shared the food they had, but at last all their stocks were exhausted, and they faced hunger and death. The village was under the curse of the spirit of the lake, who prevented the ice and snow and cold from giving way to spring.

Finally, the princess makes the great decision: without telling the villagers what she plans to do, she sacrifices herself to the spirit of the lake. All we hear is her voice offstage, as she is lost to sight in the frozen landscape. And suddenly, miraculously, the landscape is transformed into green fields and meadows with flowers and trees and birds.

The story was simple, but it evoked strong and deep feelings. And this was popular Buddhism at its best.

Many have the impression that Buddhism is a self-centered religion, a higher form of cultivation of the self, which does not care whether the world goes to ruin, provided only that the self can attain inner peace and enlightenment. It is of course true that a religion that seeks the innermost nature of the human person *can* immure its adherents in an isolated obsession with the self, and Christians too continually yield to the temptation to make the little world of their ego the center of all things: *my* experiences, *my* relationship to God, *my* eternal bliss. But a self-centered Christianity is a denial of the gospel; in the same way, a self-seeking Buddhism is a distortion of Buddhism.

One of Buddhism's primary concerns is to unmask the illusion of an immutable core in the ego. All suffering is generated by a blinded clinging to the false ego. The true human being is the one who has seen through the false world we build up around ourselves. The world of the ego is smashed to pieces, and one discovers oneself as part of a larger universe.

We can make the point with another metaphor: the ego-person is a note that enjoys its own self in isolation from the music, but the true human person discovers the self and meaning as one note in a great symphony that dies as an ego-note and rises to new life in the totality of the symphony. It possesses its life only thanks to others and in connection with others.

This is why the highest ideal in Eastern Buddhism is not the ascetic who has attained his goal and then enjoys an untroubled peace outside the cycle of transmigrating souls. The ideal is the one who has attained enlightenment but is willing to renounce the peace of his own soul and chooses to return to the world with its desires and its pain. How can one enjoy bliss for oneself, when the condemned of the earth are blinded and wander around in suffering and in darkness?

A bodhisattva is such a person who gives up his or her own salvation in order to help the helpless. In the world of mythology, these are the saints who have achieved perfection after immensely lengthy periods of asceticism and self-discipline, but like Kannon then choose to embrace the distress of the world with ears and eyes open. They are worshiped throughout the East as divine helpers. But the same is true in the world of reality, where some of the great masters leave their distant monasteries and turn up on streets and market squares, sitting among the homeless and poor people, playing with children, and sharing their insights with those they meet. There are also nameless popular "saints" who themselves are not aware that they are putting into practice the bodhisattva ideal. They are gold in the dirt of the streets, a lotus in a muddy puddle.

Perhaps not so surprising, then, that so many intuitively grasp the heart of the Gospel: God's love, which leads him to offer his life. Many find Jesus' life a radiant model of all they have dreamed of, all they have sought. He is the grain of wheat that bears fruit because it fell into the earth and died. He lived the love that freely gives its life for others. His work was fulfilled when he died on a cross. The Christian church and everything connected with it—church buildings and dogmas, ecclesiastical structures and rituals—are experienced as an imported religion with a foreign, alien taste and smell; but Jesus walks directly out of the pages of the gospels, across the boundaries of the church, and into the religious reality of the East.

One of the great Buddhist reformers in the modern period offers a very dramatic expression of this intuitive love for Jesus. Enryo Inoue began his reforming work in the 1880s, in a period when Japan was almost drowning in a wave of Westernization. The West was the model in every field, from technology and the army and education to cooking, fashions, and social conventions. Christianity was admired as the spiritual basis of the superior West, and was acclaimed as the future religion of Japan; people streamed to the churches. It was in this period that the word *ribaibaru* entered the Japanese language, from the English religious term "revival." But those who were conscious of their Japanese identity were afraid that Japan would perish and lose its own specific nature if it "sold itself" to the West.

Inoue threw himself into the struggle for the soul of Japan. He proclaimed that Buddhism was the only spiritual force that could save Japan from cultural and religious destruction. He turned his strongest weapons on Christianity, in book after book and pamphlet after pamphlet, claiming that Christianity was not only in conflict with science and sound reason but had allied itself with the great powers in the West in order to undermine the traditions of the East. Christianity was a wicked religion that must be extirpated if Japan and the East were to survive.

And yet, this fanatical anti-Christian rabble-rouser had a strange fondness for Jesus. He fought tooth and nail to destroy Christianity, but at the same time he confessed that he not only respected Jesus, but loved him: "Oh, I feel myself one with Jesus! Oh, Jesus is my brother. . . . Oh, Jesus is my faithful friend!"

The words in this brief declaration of love are extraordinarily powerful. It is not a matter of course for a Japanese to admit that he loves anything at all, and it is exceedingly surprising that a Buddhist who wishes to eradicate Christianity should "love" Jesus!

Many Buddhists share Inoue's feelings. The aggressive campaign against Christianity has virtually disappeared by now, but most Buddhists have little appreciation of traditional Christianity and its preaching; they find it incomprehensible that intellectually gifted persons should base their lives on Christianity. These reservations vanish in the case of Jesus, however: he challenges them and disturbs them. He touches something they think they recognize in their own visions. He draws on springs of water from which they themselves have drunk. In Jesus, they encounter a master who shows the path to a true and genuine life. Jesus is detached from the Christian church, walks out of the gospels, and becomes one of their own masters. He becomes a bodhisattva. "We Buddhists are ready to accept Christianity," wrote Masaharu Anesaki, one of the pioneers of the science of religion in Japan. "Indeed, our belief in Buddha is belief in Christ. We see Christ, because we see Buddha!"

Anesaki called Christianity the religion of hope. Even Jesus' last words on the cross—"My God, my God, why have you forsaken me?"—were borne up by his absolute faith in God. Christ came to lead us away from the desire that makes us cling to ourselves and to set us free to love God.

One of the most prominent Buddhist poets in the twentieth century, Momozo Kurata (1891–1943), was deeply inspired by Christ. His well-known novel *The Master and His Disciples* tells of Shinran Shonin, the thirteenth-century Buddhist reformer who is sometimes called "Buddhism's Luther." Although there can be no doubt that the book has a Buddhist message, it also shows clear traces of the author's love of Christ. This love finds its clearest expression in the letters he wrote in 1915, the year before he published the famous novel. His words about love and sacrifice still retain something of the naked vulnerability that made such a strong appeal when they were written: "I have understood how senseless it is to speak of love, if one does not know that love necessarily becomes a cross." Most people believe that they can love without renouncing their own selves. But how can one receive the Holy Spirit without sacrificing one's selfish wishes? "If I do not sacrifice all my own wishes on God's altar, all my actions are mere imperfect halves. This is what Christ's cross means. You cannot love others unless you yourself first die."

Kurata's interpretation of love and the cross can be found in many variations in modern Buddhist thinkers who see Jesus' life as the realization of the Buddhist idea that true life arises where the ego dies. They read the hymn in praise of Christ in the letter to the Philippians (2:6-8) as a poetic description of the path God took when he renounced his own self:

> Though he was in the form of God,
> he did not regard equality with God
> as something to be exploited,
> but emptied himself,
> taking the form of a slave,
> being born in human likeness. . . .
> He humbled himself
> and became obedient to the point of death—
> even death on a cross.

The Greek word *kenoun*, employed in this text, means literally to "empty out"; from this comes the word *kenosis*, a radical expression for the self-lowering in which Jesus "emptied himself" of his divine status. Modern Buddhists see Christ's "emptying out" as the deepest expression of God's innermost being. This selfless love is the emptying out of his divinity.

Accordingly, Jesus really does have some close friends among Buddhists in Japan. Some think of themselves as travelers who are en route to the Christian faith but who can never become Christians. To "become Christians" in the traditional understanding of this term would imprison them in a system where

Christ himself is held captive, i.e., the Christian church with its foreign forms of worship, organization, and doctrine. They prefer to remain en route. They are Christ's non-Christian friends who seek him outside the church.

From the church's perspective, one is, of course, entitled to query their interpretation of Christ. He is their friend and master, one who has attained enlightenment, a bodhisattva; but they have no sympathy with the church's teaching. The incarnation and Jesus' life, his death and resurrection are not regarded as salvific events, but as unique models of the sacrifice love requires. The path that Jesus took becomes meaningful only when one follows him.

If one adheres to the church's doctrine, such a position is doubtless inadequate. And yet, we cannot doubt that Jesus' non-Christian friends remind the church of something it has often forgotten, namely, the summons to *follow* Jesus. The hymn in praise of Christ is not an isolated block without relation to the rest of the letter to the Philippians: it is quoted precisely in order to call the Christian community to have "the same mind" as Christ himself.

Let us add one further point. By making Jesus their friend and master, Buddhists have taken him out of the church and the context that made him an alien Western import. They have discovered that he also belongs to the East—or rather, that his life and death break through all borders and call to everyone who belongs to the truth.

Mission and Roots

Every now and again, we hear the old allegation that mission destroys roots, that it tears people out of the context in which they live and makes them foreigners in their own culture. What gives Christians the right to destroy the way other people and other religions see themselves? And when will Christians grasp how their missionary work is seen by those who are outside the church?

Some time ago a newspaper article argued that the attempt to communicate the Christian message slices through "roots that are absolutely essential, if life is to be lived in all its fullness. People become rootless and homeless. The deep sensation of belonging to a fellowship is put at risk, and people are left with a feeling of grief at the loss of something valuable and important."

We cannot refuse to grapple with the questions posed by the critics of Christian mission. Naturally, the supporters of missionary work are quick to defend it, saying that this is ultimately a question of obeying Jesus' commandment to make all the nations his disciples (cf. Matt 28:19-20), and that mission involves a spiritual battle between good and evil. But these answers are inadequate, for it is a fact that Christian mission has often torn people out of the existential context in which they lived, making them foreigners vis-à-vis their own culture. The attempt to give them a new identity has detached them from their roots and made them homeless in their own hearts. If the Christian faith does not help someone achieve a true relationship to his or her own self, it will always be borrowed goods, a foreign body that can threaten personal development. Faith is meant to make people whole, not to make them spiritual refugees nourished on values borrowed from others.

To draw the conclusion that conversion from one religion to another is necessarily a bad thing would, however, indicate a simplistic understanding of de facto historical processes, as well as a failure to appreciate the unease that always accompanies the religious search. Every people and culture knows periods of radical religious transformations when religious allegiance changes: old ideas are discarded or lose their power and are replaced by new ideas. The same is true of individuals. Some rebel against their parents' faith, or faith can quite simply die, or perhaps they encounter a faith that is more meaningful than their old faith. This leads to fear, pain, and grief, but this is often a necessary process in a healthy human life. One does not lose one's own identity when one rebels against inherited values, nor when one casts away something that has ceased to be meaningful.

I doubt whether there is anyone who can retain *all* his roots. Some roots are diseased; roots can be destroyed by lack of nutrients or water. And roots can be cut by external circumstances. Sometimes roots must be dug up and planted in new soil if they are to have access to life-giving water. All this applies to religious faith as well. Many people have had to cut through Christian roots that had been destroyed in a diseased and acidic soil in order to discover their true selves. Others again find that the Christian faith allows them, for the first time in their lives, to put down roots and connect with their deepest longings.

But we must note that whatever the individual circumstances, it is impossible to have a whole relationship to oneself unless one has a living relationship to one's past. We can try to reject the past, suppress it, or forget it, but it does not go away: sooner or later, it will emerge with its demands. We must work on our past and integrate it—positively or negatively—into the life we live in the present and the future.

Christian mission is rightly criticized because it often demands a break with what went before, without recognizing that much of the past was good, that God may have been present in it, and that most of the roots were good. This is why it is not surprising to meet Japanese Christians who, after some years as Christians, begin to look to their past in search of connections. They have received a Christian identity, but they discover that the faith cannot be wholly their own unless they establish a genuine relationship to their past. In some cases, this leads them away from the Christian faith, which had never really been more than borrowed goods. But if their faith is genuine, the rediscovery of their roots leads to a new richness and freedom—freedom for a new meeting with that which belongs to the past. Some of this will indeed be rejected, but all that is "true, good, and honorable" takes on a new meaning. The past is not an empty space, but a source of richness and joy.

My question is whether the Christian church is entitled to engage in mission, as long as it remains unable to preserve the good things in the cultures in which it works. Is it meaningful to work as a missionary—yet not ask oneself in all seriousness what place the religions and cultures one encounters have in God's plan? What are the insights, the truth, and the goodness with which God has endowed them? How can other religions and cultures help to deepen our Christian insight and experience? And how can the Christian message be communicated in a way that preserves all that is valuable? Non-Christians often feel that they have to break out of their own culture in order to become disciples of Jesus; but can this be right?

God did not create us in a vacuum, so to speak: he poured out his gifts on all peoples. Many Norwegian supporters of missionary work have still to grasp what it means to see every people and nation "with God's eyes," appreciating their special gifts and radiance, as they sing in a famous missionary hymn.

If Christian missionary work is to have the right to summon people to become Jesus' disciples, it must first learn to appreciate what is going on in the depths of other religions and cultures. This entails sensitivity to those roots that are necessary "if life is to be lived in all its fullness and meaning."

Disciples and Hangers-on

Jesus knew two forms of mission. He rejected one of them but commanded the disciples to dedicate their lives to the other: Jesus wanted disciples, not hangers-on.

He was supremely harsh in his description of that type of mission that sought to produce copies of the missionary. He castigated the Pharisees and scribes: "You cross sea and land to make a single convert, and you make the new convert twice as much a child of hell as yourselves" (Matt 23:15). He himself called people to discipleship and then sent them out in their turn to make "all nations" his disciples (Matt 28:18-20).

A disciple is one who has met a master. A good master possesses insight and experience of life, and the disciples are formed by seeing and hearing him and by living in the master's presence. They become his apprentices, just as Jesus himself had been his Father's apprentice. He was not interested in producing copies of himself—he wanted persons who were alive. The master has a message to communicate, but he does not want it to be learned by rote. His message must take shape in the disciples' lives, so that it can set them free and help them to grow. "You will know the truth, and the truth will make you free" (John 8:32).

A bad master will have only hangers-on who cling to him because he has something they themselves lack. They become dependent on his every movement; he must direct their lives and tell them what they have to do. They are captives, without liberty or the chance to develop. They do what the master does, but without knowing why. They say what he says, but without knowing what the words mean. They are copies, mere marionettes in a puppet theater.

A bad master says: "Come here, and become like us!" He needs hangers-on who support his cause and follow his slogans. The result is a smoothed-out uniformity that holds them captive.

A good master says: "Come here, and get to know life. Live life in all its richness, and share it with others." He wants disciples who elaborate their teaching in their own encounter with life. The ideal is not uniformity but fellowship and plurality. The good master teaches a truth that sets people free and promotes their growth and development.

The Spark

One of my first tasks after completing my course in the Japanese language was to discuss religious questions with five or six pupils in the agricultural college run by the mission. This allowed me to have close contacts with young Japanese, and I soon discovered that they knew nothing at all about religion. They came from Tokyo and Osaka and other big cities and could not find one single word to express their own or their families' faith. They knew that they were Buddhists, and they remembered roughly to which branch of Buddhism they belonged. They had taken part in religious ceremonies at regular intervals. But that was all.

I prepared myself thoroughly for the lessons. We studied the principal ideas in Christianity for a number of weeks, and they were certainly not uninterested—they made notes in their books and asked questions. But no spark set them alight. It seemed that there was no connection between Christianity and their lives.

Things began to happen when we turned to Buddhism. These secularized young Japanese, who had no idea what they believed, suddenly woke to life. They themselves were not able to formulate Buddhist ideas, but when I—a Christian missionary—supplied them with words and concepts, the words began to come alive. We visited a local Buddhist temple together and participated in the monks' meditation. They saw connections that they had never seen before. This did not mean that they became active Buddhists, but they discovered that this belonged to them, this was where they were at home.

I must admit that I was a little disappointed. Had I made such a bad job of communicating the life that lies in Christianity? And was Buddhism so deeply rooted that even secularized young people felt at home in it? My initial humbling was soon replaced by a sense of wonder, however, as I reflected on the situation of Christianity in Japan.

Christianity came to Japan as part of a new age, and it has played a much more central role than Buddhism in forming modern society. Christians were actively involved in working to establish democracy in Japan. They fought against social injustice and discrimination and promoted the rights of women. They made socialism a political alternative. They saw the vision of a new Japan. Experiences from the West made Christians much better prepared to encounter the challenge of secularization and tendencies critical of religion. They took it for granted that Buddhism and the ancestral religions would draw the shorter straw in the encounter with the modern world.

In many ways, Christianity has a strong position in Japan. Studies show that many who have never set their foot inside a church esteem Christianity more highly than the other religions. Christianity may perhaps seem a little eccentric and foreign, but people associate it above all with positive values such as love, care for others, and justice. Optimists interpret people's positive attitude to Christianity as a sign that it has a great potential in Japan.

And yet, so little happens. Christianity encounters well-wishers who are interested and listen to the message; but the traditional preaching rarely kindles a spark that sets people alight. There is a great gulf between Christianity and the traditional consciousness. The pupils at the agricultural college humbled my missionary ambitions with their polite rejection of Christianity and their intuitive appreciation of a Buddhism they did not know. At the same time, however, they also opened my eyes to what was going on below the surface of people's lives.

Buddhism is undergoing a serious crisis in Japanese society, perhaps even graver than that of Christianity in the West. But Buddhism lives on and in a hidden manner forms people's questions and existential attitudes. It touches their despair and their longings. Buddhism is present when life's riddles are to be solved. If one offers explanations and answers to life's questions *without* touching this hidden life, there will be no spark to ignite others. If Japanese Christianity is to have a future, it must encounter people on the deepest level.

Fidelity

It was not expected that a woman secretary would have opinions about her work—she was to do what she was employed to do, without asking questions. But "Haruko" had not been at the study center for long before we realized that she was different from most young Japanese women. She asked questions, and she had her own points of view. And not least: she presented her views with vigor! She protested against working conditions and her salary, and she commented on the plans for seminars and series of lectures. She found the academic and religious worlds intolerably male-dominated. She corrected the men's manuscripts when they got too tortuous and incomprehensible.

It was only when it came to religion that she fell silent. Her words became vague and evasive, for this was something she did not understand. Indeed, it seemed as if she had no interest in religion at all, which was somewhat surprising in view of the fact that she had applied on her own initiative for a job in our institute for the study of Japanese religion. In the course of the years, she heard a large number of lectures by Christian leaders, Buddhist philosophers, Shinto priests, and leaders of cults. But she never gave any hint of her own stance.

It took ten years for her to disclose where she stood on religious matters. This happened when a rather aggressive Buddhist lecturer attempted to force her to take a position: "You have to say where you stand! But perhaps you are like so many other young people, just not interested in religion!" Her answer came in a flash, with a severity that almost made us fall out of our seats: "I have my own religion, but I am not going to discuss it with outsiders!"

A few days later, she told me about her faith. She came from a humble rural background, and her parents belonged to a new monotheistic religion called Konkokyo, founded more than a hundred years earlier by a popular prophet who claimed that he had received divine revelations. He preached a simple faith in God, and practiced his faith in preaching, intercessory prayer, and spiritual direction. His religion gradually spread over the whole country, but it still has no more than a few hundred thousand members.

"It is not all that impressive," she said. "No visions that take heaven by storm, no profound philosophy." At the study center, she had come into contact with much more challenging religions. Highly trained theologians and philosophers drew on traditions that were thousands of years old and introduced her to vast, exciting landscapes. The religion of her parents seemed a poor affair in comparison to Buddhism and Christianity.

"It is like comparing the little hillside behind my childhood home with the gigantic beauty of Mount Fuji," she said. "Fuji towers up in its lonely majesty, admired and adored. People write songs about it. But there are not many who have ever heard of my hill. And yet, I have come to realize in the course of these years where I belong. *My* home lies at the foot of my childhood hill. I left, because I wanted to get away and see something of the world. I have seen a lot, and learned a lot. I have admired Mount Fuji and other stupendous landscapes. But that is not where I belong."

We fell silent after she had spoken. She had drawn the veil aside and uncovered something of the secrets of her own life, and I understood that I had to tread cautiously.

A few months later, her father became sick, and she gave up her job and went home to look after her elderly parents. As a missionary, I ought perhaps to have been disappointed that she had not become a Christian, although we had worked together for ten years; but I was left with a feeling of admiration and gratitude. She had chosen the modest hillside of her childhood home in preference to the imposing summit of Mount Fuji. She gave up the challenges of the great city, and chose the simple life of her parents. Perhaps that was where she was meant to be. At any rate, she taught me something very important about belonging. And about fidelity.

"I Want to Be a Japanese"

According to one historian, there is no conscious apostasy among Japanese Christians: they do not break with the church and remove their name from the parish registers but simply withdraw silently. They disappear through the back door and are gone.

I assumed that something like this was happening in "Noriko's" life. I had met her during my first year in Japan. Like most high school students, she wanted to learn English; at the same time, she was looking for something, perhaps an alternative to the inherited patterns of gender roles, which did not always attract the younger women. Through Christianity, she came into contact with something else, something that did indeed seem foreign, yet also appealed to her and attracted her.

After a while, she was baptized. The pastor reported that she was actively involved in church services and Bible study. She was one of the core in her little community, where she played the organ and was a member of the parish council.

When she got married, there was less time for church activities. The pattern is familiar: the husband sees the church as a rival and asks why his wife should squander her time on the church instead of making things nice for him on Sunday, the one day when he is at home. The children too make their demands, and it is not his job to look after them. Often, women stay away from the church for many years, until their children have grown up. Only then can they come to Sunday worship with a good conscience.

One day, Noriko turned up in church. She said that she had been thinking things over for a long time and wanted to talk about something important. She had decided to leave the church. When I asked what had led to this decision, she replied in a voice that was low and cautious yet surprisingly strong: "I want to be a Japanese!"

She was now living out in the countryside, and wanted to be a part of village life. I asked if this necessarily meant breaking with Christianity. "I have never really had a deep faith," she replied. "I was attracted by Christianity because it represented something different. There was a romantic glow about the church— something foreign and new. And then, I got the chance to learn English." Her gaze wavered a little, before she continued: "The warmth and fellowship in the church were wonderful. But perhaps I have never really grasped what 'faith' means."

Now she was back in Japanese society, where she belonged— with her neighbors, with a Japanese piety that permeated the rhythm of the year and the various phases of life. "I want to be a Japanese!"

Our conversation lasted a long time. Perhaps she was right to state that her faith had never gone very deep? What was I supposed to say—that she nevertheless had been in contact with something that she would never wholly shake off? That God would still be present in her life, even if she did not think so much about that fact? That the door would always be open for her, and that we would accompany her in our thoughts and prayers?

I do not remember exactly what I said; probably my words ran along these lines. And I thanked her for many years of friendship. The friendship would certainly continue!

This was one of the last conversations I had in Japan. The words stayed with me as an abiding reminder of the vulnerable situation of Christianity in that country. At the same time, it struck me that in one way Noriko had perhaps been more deeply influenced by Christianity than she realized, namely, in her need for openness and truthfulness. As I have mentioned, most people simply disappear silently through the back door; but Noriko left with her head held high, leaving the church the same way she had entered, the main entrance. That door remains open. Maybe she will go in by that door again one day.

A Larger Pattern

The Christian faith had given Akiko something to live for. She was pulled out of the anonymous mass of students and received a face and a name. Friends and church activities gave her life a new meaning and direction. Jesus was a tangible reality for her. On the wall hung the characters that summarized what she had experienced: "God is love."

She had not in fact experienced any break with her past. She came from a home where religion was unimportant. It shed a radiance over the cares and crises of life—birth and childhood, weddings and funerals—but she did not understand the monotonous recitation of the Buddhist priest, and the prayers of the Shinto priest were a voice from past centuries. Religious life in her home was largely the responsibility of a pious grandmother.

Her family had not protested when she was baptized. They thought that Christianity was a good religion. This allowed her to close the book of her past with a good conscience. The past had lost its meaning: now life was beginning.

After she had been active in the church for many years, Akiko's past caught up with her. She felt rootless and restless, with an unclear sensation of living in a vacuum. She had heard that people who had had a leg amputated often felt pain in the leg that had been removed; and Akiko felt pain in the roots that had been cut off. When she was present at religious ceremonies, she felt drawn to the old ways. She thought of her grandmother's warm piety. The recitations of the Buddhist priest allowed her to sense a mystery, and Buddhist sacred texts both disturbed her and attracted her.

Her inner tensions continued for a while, but then she began to investigate her past. When she did so, her life gained wholeness and richness. Her childhood and adolescence came back to her with a wealth of memories, and she realized that much of the past had been good. She rediscovered insights and experiences that had pointed her toward a more authentic life. She also saw much that had rightly disappeared from her life—yet even things that were of no consequence, or things that were downright useless, were part of the total story of her life. She could not erase them without eliminating something of her own self.

There were probably few who noticed that something was happening in Akiko's life, since everything went on as normal. Her prayers were the same, and she continued faithfully to attend church. But she felt more secure. She saw a larger pattern. God had not entered her life only on the day she was baptized as a twenty-year-old; he had woven his images into her childhood and adolescence. In the Christian faith, her past acquired a new meaning. The memories of her grandmother's piety filled her with gratitude. The Buddhist texts and recitations no longer disturbed her, but took on meaning as a part of the story of her soul. As a person, she became more whole, and the characters on her wall took on new life: "God is love."

The Outward Path
and the Homeward Path—
Toward a Greater Faith

The borders are widened and the world opens up

when we leave home

and begin to travel.

How can one live in the borderland

without becoming homeless?

For some, the outward path

also becomes the homeward path;

but the journey leaves its traces on their soul.

The house to which they return

is different from the house they left.

God is the same—yet so different.

Faith is nourished by the same sources,

but it seeks a greater wholeness and more space.

*"Kikyô" means to return to one's native village,
to the starting point of the human person.*

KIKYÔ

". . . the love you had at first."
(Revelation 2:4)

*"Show me the face you had
before you were born!"*
(Buddhist saying)

A Modern Pilgrim

Once upon a time, there lived a Jew in Krakow, Eisik, son of Jekel. He was told in a dream to search for a treasure under the bridge that led to the royal palace in Prague. Eisik left home and went all the way to Prague, but he did not dare to dig, for fear of the watchman on the bridge. But he stayed faithfully by the bridge day by day, until the captain of the guard noticed him and asked what he was looking for.

Eisik told him about the dream that had led him the long way from a distant country. The captain laughed at the naïve Jew who had set out on his travels for the sake of a dream. He himself had once had a similar dream, he said: he was to search for a treasure under the oven in the house of a Jew in Krakow called Eisik, son of Jekel.

"I can just see myself tearing down all the houses in a city where half of the Jews are called Eisik, and the other half Jekel!" said the captain, and laughed again.

Eisik bowed his farewell, returned to his home, excavated the treasure, and a built a house of prayer called the School of Reb Eisik Reb Jekel.

Eisik's dream led him to a far distant country in search of a treasure. There he heard the dream of another person and discovered the treasure that lay hidden in his own living room. Perhaps most people bear a dream within themselves; and some actually leave home to find the treasure they have seen in their dreams. Hundreds of thousands of modern Westerners have searched for treasures in foreign religions. Many have set out on their travels to India, Nepal, southeast Asia, or Japan to find a faith superior to the humdrum Christianity they knew from their childhood home. Some found treasures in the course of their journey and never returned home; some perished; others came back even poorer than when they had left. But some returned, and found the treasure in their own living room.

I met Eisik in Kyoto—an American who had bid farewell to his childhood home and all its works and all its ways. He had refused military service in Vietnam and had rejected violence and the consumer society. This necessarily entailed rejection of the religion that was consumed as part of the American way of life. The clichés and cheap explanations he was offered undermined what was left of his Christian faith. He had to get away if he was to save his soul.

His dream took him to Japan. He sensed that there were hidden treasures in Zen Buddhism, and he hoped to find the great enlightenment in meditation, a boundary-breaking experience of reality. Here he met a master who was willing to guide him. Morning and evening, he took part in *Zazen*, meditation in a sitting posture. He sat through periods of meditation that lasted from early morning to late at night, interrupted only by small pauses and simple meals. The discipline was unyielding, and his body ached. But he was willing to sacrifice everything, if only he could find the treasure.

One day, as he sat in deep concentration in the meditation hall, he had the greatest shock of his life. Suddenly, he knew with a certainty that vibrated in every fiber of his being: "I am a Christian!" The treasure for which he was looking lay hidden in the living room he had left behind him. The Christianity that he had rejected became a new reality, something tremendously close to him. The treasure had been there all along, but he had to go to a foreign country in order to discover it.

Eisik excavated the treasure and built a house of prayer. My friend too became a man of prayer, one who brought light to others. This was probably a reflection of the treasure he had found, but the journey itself had also given him light. His dreams and travels lived on in his life. The room to which he returned was not the closed world of his childhood home. His journey had left its mark on him, and he now lived in an open universe. His faith had been deepened by what he had seen. He continued to meditate, and he still listened to the wisdom of the Zen master. The more he penetrated Zen, the more clearly did he see the treasures of the Christian faith.

Like a true Christian, he discovered that "in [him] are hidden all the treasures of wisdom and knowledge" (Col 2:3).

When the Borders Become Too Narrow

We were at the meeting place. It was born of the farsighted in-spiration of Scandinavian missionaries who wanted Christians and Buddhists to encounter one another on the deep level. They built an institution in the classic Chinese style on a hilltop out-side Hong Kong and called it Tao Fong Shan, the Mountain of the Dao-wind or Christ-wind. Its white buildings, with their blue-black tiles and red pillars, are hidden in the cool shadows cast by evergreens. It is an oasis in all the turmoil of the teem-ing metropolis.

For more than seventy years, this place has nourished the dream of making Christ's presence visible in the East. The path of Christ and the path of Buddha must intersect, and something new must come into being at the place where they meet.

Here, two of my friends told about their own paths. We had sat together in intense discussions for several days. A handful of Bud-dhists and Christians from eastern Asia had come together to seek deeper understanding and insight, and we spoke of the potential of religion to create reconciliation and peace. Dreams were born; thoughts took form. It was challenging and exciting, but perhaps a little abstract, until Thomas brought us back to earth.

He had grown up in a Christian family and had himself played an active role in church life. It was almost symbolic that he should have been given the baptismal name "Thomas" in addition to his Korean name because his mind was divided—it was hard to be a Korean and a Christian simultaneously.

His path led him away from the church. He had sought his spiritual roots, looking into the past to find a context in which he could live. He felt a strong attraction to Buddhism and began to read its sacred texts. Here there was much for him to learn, and his ideas grew in depth and perspective.

In this period of upheaval, his Christian friends and guides told him that he must abandon his interest in Buddhism, since its sacred texts were dangerous. In the end, he was forced to choose between Buddhism and Christianity. The church had no place for a Christian with Buddhist sympathies.

Accordingly, he left the church, and studied Buddhism instead of Christian theology. He became a learned Buddhist, but his faith was not a closed world, since he held that faith is much more than "believing in something." Faith means devoting oneself to the truth. His Buddhism was a relationship to reality, a way of existing.

Early one morning, I slipped away from the stress of the conference to celebrate Holy Communion in a little community close by. Five or six people were assembled around the Lord's table in a small room—and Thomas was one of them.

Boundaries were shattered as we sat together in the simple room and received the Lord's Body and Blood. Thomas had been forced out of the church because he was seeking a path into Buddhism. But he was present in the chapel because he loved Christ. The walls disappeared, and the cramped room expanded. Thomas the Buddhist was still one of Jesus' disciples.

On the following day, another participant told his story, and this too involved breaking through boundaries. He had grown up in a Christian family in Sri Lanka, in a solidly Hindu environment. His mother died when he was very small, and his father had to work hard to feed himself and his numerous children. This meant that my friend spent most of his time as a child with the neighbors, who were all Hindus. Every Sunday, however, the father gathered the family together, and they went faithfully to the church in the neighboring village.

Problems gradually emerged as he began to understand what the pastor was talking about—for the sermon often dealt with Christianity and paganism. Daily life in that region supplied the pastor with plenty of material for a description of Hindu thinking and worship, and he castigated their idolatry, superstition, and remoteness from reality. Christians must be on their guard, lest they get entangled in the religious past. They had crossed over from darkness to light, and they must make a clear distinction between God and Satan.

My friend could make no sense of all of this. He had seen how his Hindu neighbors lived, and he could not accept the idea that they were in darkness. There were indeed customs and ideas unacceptable to Christians, but had he not also seen a kind of divine presence in their impoverished existence?

Finally the crisis came, and he had to choose. He must either deny God or find him in a new way. He could not continue to believe in a God who kept himself detached from the everyday life of the Hindus, for it was precisely there that he himself had experienced love and care. He did not want anything to do with a stingy God. At the end of this process, he rediscovered God. He received a new vision of the Creator who loves the world and who does not allow himself to be shut in behind church walls and religious boundaries, but has permitted people to live over the face of the whole earth "so that they would search for God and perhaps grope for him and find him" (Acts 17:27).

Theological Addresses

Norwegian addresses are simple and clear. No one can be in any doubt about where I live: Lilac Road 12, 0870 Oslo. The street has a curve, but forms a line from its beginning to its end: 8-10-12. And that is where I live. Everything is perfectly clear.

This is how we tend to think of "theological addresses"—one is a Christian, one is a Lutheran, and the path is a straightforward line that does not veer to either side, either toward Catholicism and catholicizing tendencies to the right, or to Reformed and enthusiastic tendencies on the left. No, we simply take the path, 8-10-12, and that is where we live.

After a few years in Japan, one learns to take one's bearings in another manner. One does not live on a street where the house numbers follow one another in serried ranks: one lives in an area, and the smallest unit is often a few blocks of houses. There is no point in giving a taxi driver an address and expecting him to find the house. He would no doubt find the area where you live, but if you are to get any closer, you must take your bearings by means of prominent and well-known places in the neighborhood—a school, a tower, a temple, a church. To begin with, this is confusing, but after a while it functions perfectly.

This applies to my theological address in Japan too. My faith is not seen as a house on one particular street, one point on a line that can be isolated from its surroundings. My faith acquires its meaning on the basis of the area where I live. The building nearest to me is a church. It may be rather a poor building, but it remains the most important point of orientation. A little farther on, across the street, is a Buddhist temple, and there are a number of neighbors in the area who give my existence color and meaning.

Those who are used to the addresses of roads and streets in Norway are initially confused and irritated at my area address. They want to find the way to my house without paying heed to the surroundings, and they think it a hopeless task to get one's bearings on the basis of a larger area. But gradually, they discover that their accustomed way of thinking about people's addresses reduces the perspective, and they begin to sense that area addresses may be more sensible, since these include the neighbors and integrate them into a meaningful context.

Let me say a little about my Japanese neighbors. The church that dominates our neighborhood is Lutheran, and it is the obvious point of orientation for those who want to find the way. It is in a bad state of repair and makes a rather sad impression. Its doors and windows are closed and locked for most of the week, and even on Sundays only a handful of people come to worship. But in the depth of my heart, I know that this church is my spiritual home. I would have been rootless without it. Indeed, I love it. Perhaps it can open its windows and doors one day and become young again?

The church may be sufficient as a point of orientation, but it is natural to mention the Buddhist temple too. To be quite honest, things would have looked pretty poor around here without it—it is the pride and joy of our neighborhood, an expression of people's need to create a space for the sacred, and a monument to one of the richest spiritual traditions in the East. I am not so impressed by what goes on in the temple. The priest's work is limited basically to liturgies for the dead, funerals, and administration, and those who come to worship can seldom explain what it is they really believe in. But I have looked behind the façade and studied the history of the traditions, and I have discovered hidden treasures of religious experience and insight that have gradually left their mark on the way I myself think and live as a Christian.

The other neighbors are perhaps less important. The Shinto temple has helped many to retain at least a rudimentary appreciation of the mystery of nature, a nameless sense of a divine presence. Some of my friends belong to the new religions, modern revival movements that spring out of the inherited popular religion. Their doctrine and preaching can seem banal and superficial, but my friends never tire of reminding me that a faith that remains close to their life and can transform their daily living is more important than a high-flown philosophy that does not touch their daily lives.

Most of my neighbors have little connection with religion at all. It is not that they are against religion, but that it has no meaning for them. They appear to get on perfectly well without it, and thus they remind me of one of those puzzles to which I never find the solution: if faith is the most decisively important thing in life, how can people get on so well without it?

My Japanese area address has taught me that theology means more than just locating oneself at one clear point on a line. Theology must be lived in a larger context. Faith is formed not only by drawing boundary lines vis-à-vis one's surroundings. Rather, faith takes shape when our neighbors become a part of our life.

Toward a Larger Faith

Every time I have wandered around in the borderland and reached summits where I had a panoramic view of the landscape in all directions, I have been forced to ask: can I exclude any of this? Is not this the world of *my* faith? Some tell me that I must reject the border zone and return home; others think that I must forget my own Christian faith in order to lead a full life on the far side of the border. This choice is impossible! If faith should demand that I forget the border zone, it would be too narrow. But if I were to cross the border for good and put down my roots in a foreign region, I would be consumed by homesickness. Faith would become rootless.

This is why I sought a larger faith. My travels in the border zone between East and West kindled in me the longing for a faith large enough to encompass all I had seen and experienced both in my homeland and in the borderland, a faith that would lead me through new landscapes, with space enough for life in all its contradictory variety.

A larger faith does not close the borders but throws them open. A larger faith does not claim that it has God under lock and key in its own world but sees God's tracks everywhere. A larger faith grows out of the profession of faith in the Creator of heaven and earth.

I crossed the border in order to bring God to new worlds—but I discovered that God was already there. And naturally enough! How could he not be present in the world that was his own? It was he who blew the breath of life into the human person's nostrils so that Adam became a living being. How could one fail to perceive God's presence when the breath of life became deep and the heart beat strongly? All I could do was to point: There he is! Look! And not least: I could point to the place, the time, and the person where God's own being and work shone out in transfigured splendor, namely, Jesus Christ.

I have never understood how some people can use Christ to erect borders. They think that their profession of faith in him means that the circle closes around him, with a clear difference between that which is inside the circle and that which is outside. And yet Jesus broke through borders all his life! He was in places where no one expected him to be! He never let himself be imprisoned in the categories of the pious, but made God present where he really ought not to have been present—if he had been a "pious" God. Jesus kept on surprising me by turning up on the little side streets, far away from all the paths that led to a church building.

Perhaps we are wrong in the way we conceive the center and the periphery of the circle. Ought not a faith that is truly centered on Christ have the same openness that he displayed? Concentration on *this* center frees us from the need to define the periphery of the circle; on the contrary, we perceive how the light radiates out from Christ to the uttermost borders of the circle, permeating everything.

A larger faith takes seriously the Bible's affirmation that "everything" was created in Christ, through him, and for him. "Everything" means all that is in the universe, "in heaven and on earth . . . things visible and invisible, whether thrones and dominions or rulers or powers" (Col 1:16). And that which has been created will one day be gathered together in him (Eph 1:10). We do not fully understand what this means, and perhaps not even Paul himself understood it, for he uses mysterious words when he praises this mystery. At any rate, his words affirm that nothing in the world—with all its beauty and ugliness, its goodness and evil, its yearning for God and its devilry—is untouched by Christ and that everything can be transformed and created anew by God's grace. If Christ is involved both in the creation and in the perfecting of all things, it would be a mockery of the divine plan to close the borders and prevent him from working in the world, in those landscapes in which he in his goodness allows us to travel.

My longing for a larger faith was kindled by the divine presence I believed I discerned in the border zone of the East. It might be confusing, chaotic, and unclear, but I never doubted that God was there. I wanted to put a name to his presence and show its true nature. At the same time, the border zone left lasting impressions on my own mind, giving me a larger appreciation for the hidden mystery of his presence.

Gradually, I also realized that the border zone is not just "out there." It exists just as much here at home. The border zone is in our own mind. If we do not shut ourselves up in our faith, we cross borders all the time.

We need a faith that can accommodate human life in all its dimensions. We need a larger faith.